need to know?

Dog breeds

Robert Killick

Collins

First published in 2008 by
Collins, an imprint of
HarperCollins Publishers
77–85 Fulham Palace Road
Hammersmith, London W6 8JB

www.collins.co.uk

Collins is a registered trademark of HarperCollins Publishers Limited
11 10 09 08
6 5 4 3 2 1

A catalogue record for this book is available from the British Library.

Created by: **SP Creative Design**
Editor: **Heather Thomas**
Designer: **Rolando Ugolini**
Photographs: **Rolando Ugolini, Charlie Colmer, David Dalton and
Bruce Tanner**
Alan V. Walker K9 Photography: pages 36, 41, 45, 49, 51, 53, 55, 67,
77, 79, 81, 83, 89, 93, 95, 105, 117, 149, 161, 169, 175 and 186

ISBN: 978-0-00-726854-2

Printed and bound by **Printing Express Ltd, Hong Kong**

Dedication

This book is dedicated to my
Zoe Alicija Clarke in the fond
love dogs as much as her gra

Contents

Introduction

If you're not sure which is the right breed for you, look no further, as this is a comprehensive guide to the most popular dog breeds as well as some lesser known ones, with information on how they evolved as well as their temperament, appearance, daily care and health.

Learning about the breeds

One of the objects of this book is to acquaint you with some breeds of dog that are not so well known but which, nonetheless, will bring the same amount of companionship and undemanding affection as the more familiar breeds. Because introducing a puppy or young dog into a family is the beginning of a relationship which may last for many years, it is incumbent upon all those concerned to get it right! And that is where this useful book can help you – there is practical information on over 60 breeds.

All puppies are gorgeous and it is too easy to be influenced by those appealing little black eyes and not to consider what the dog will be like when it is fully grown. The best advice is usually to go for a pedigree dog as you will then know, within certain parameters, how big the puppy will grow, the type and colour of its coat, how much exercise and daily care it needs and, most importantly, what sort of temperament it has.

However, before making up your mind and deciding on a breed, you should reflect on your own circumstances – whether you have the time to fulfil the needs of a dog as far as grooming and exercise are concerned, and do you have enough space for the breed you are considering. All these considerations are covered in more detail in Chapter 1.

So have a look at the breed or breeds to which you may have taken a fancy. Go to a major dog show and meet the breeders and the dogs. Read this book and check out the breeds that interest and attract you. Do your homework thoroughly now and you will maximize your chances of finding the right dog for you. Good luck in your quest for a new friend.

1 Choosing the right breed

If you have decided to own a dog, impulse buying is your worst enemy – all dogs, especially puppies, are so appealing that it is easy to fall for one without thinking it out properly or considering the consequences. Buying a puppy or an adult dog is one of the most important purchases you will make. Not only will he be dependent on you for many years but you are also extending your family.

Which breed?

There is a breed of dog which is suitable for everyone, no matter what their circumstances, lifestyle, health, location or personal preferences. The UK Kennel Club registers nearly 200 breeds and you need to establish which one is right for you and your family.

must know

Pedigree dogs are classified roughly according to the type of work they do. In the UK, the groups are:
- **Hounds**
- **Gundogs**
- **Terriers**
- **Utility dogs**
- **Working dogs**
- **Pastoral (herding) dogs**
- **Toy dogs**

Location

An important consideration when choosing a dog is where you live and the size and style of your home. All dogs love freedom and while most are suitable for country living, not all breeds adapt successfully to urban life. Large, active dogs need plenty of space to run and play and thus are not suited to life in a cramped apartment in a tower block, unlike some small companion and toy breeds. Long periods of being confined in a small space may sometimes lead to boredom and behavioural problems for some breeds, especially working dogs.

Lifestyle and attitudes

Next, consider your lifestyle. Do you go out to work, full time or part time? Can you take the dog with you? If the house is left empty for long periods, is there a neighbour, friend or member of the family who can check on the dog and take him out? Are you prepared to walk and exercise the dog at least twice every day? Will you have the time to train, socialize and play with him? If you are house proud and your dog has a thick coat that tends to shed hairs, would this be a source of irritation? Are you prepared to groom the dog every day? Will other members of your family help look after the dog?

Another important factor when choosing a breed is your own personality. Are you energetic, sociable and fun-loving or are you quiet, home-loving and sedate? Do you have many visitors, go out a lot, enjoy long walks or runs? All these aspects of your temperament and lifestyle have an important bearing on the dog you choose. For example, if you don't enjoy exercise or have access to a nearby park or open countryside, you should not choose an energetic breed, such as a Border Collie or Springer Spaniel. If you love long hikes over hills and dales, don't get a Pug. If you like playing noisy, boisterous games and have a large family and circle of friends, don't buy a breed with a sensitive temperament. Try to match the breed to your personality and lifestyle.

The cost of dog ownership

The costs of buying and owning any dog can be considerable. The initial cost of purchasing a pedigree puppy depends on the breed, and some are very expensive indeed. However, even cross-breeds or mongrels still need first vaccinations, annual boosters and veterinary treatment as well as food, bedding, toys and equipment.

A fact of life is that the bigger the dog, the more he eats. A large dog can be quite expensive to feed properly, so only consider owning one if you can afford to provide sufficient quantities of a nutritious diet. Another important consideration is the cost of professional grooming, unless you are prepared to learn how to do it yourself. It can be costly to keep some breeds, such as Poodles, Airedales and Old English Sheepdogs trimmed, clipped or stripped and looking their best.

Large dog breeds, such as this German Shepherd, can be quite expensive to keep as well as demanding lots of your time.

Finding your dog

Once you have decided on a particular breed, you need to find a suitable dog, whether it's a puppy or an adult, that needs a new loving home. One of the easiest and most convenient ways to do this is by surfing the internet for useful, informative sites.

must know

Before you decide on a dog breed, think about the cost not only of buying a pedigree puppy but also the initial outlay on equipment as well as food for your dog, vet's bills and insurance. Don't buy a dog that you cannot afford to keep.

The internet

By Googling the breed that interests you or simply clicking on The Kennel Club's website or one of the breed societies or rescue organizations, you can find out more about the breed history and clubs as well as the breeders themselves. The Kennel Club will also provide details of breeders in your area, but if you have set your heart on one of the rarer breeds you may have to be prepared to travel further afield.

The media

The weekly newspapers and monthly magazines devoted to pedigree dogs, their care, exhibition and breeding are also a good source of up-to-date information on breeders and litters of puppies available. However, be wary of advertisements for puppies in local newspapers; some may be placed by unscrupulous dealers or owners of puppy farms who have no interest in the dogs' welfare or in breeding healthy puppies with good temperaments. Never buy a dog from a man in the pub or who offers to meet in a car park – you will have no 'back-up' in case of trouble and no background knowledge of the dog you are buying. It is always wise to buy direct from a breeder who should be properly licensed and recognized by The Kennel Club, or

Opposite: Cocker Spaniels are one of the world's most popular dog breeds. If you are thinking of buying a puppy, check out the breeding line to make sure that it is free of genetic anomalies.

from a registered charity. Most importantly, always insist on visiting the breeder's home and seeing the mother *in situ* with the other puppies. Check that the address on the pedigree papers matches the address that you visit to view the puppies.

Local sources

The staff in your local veterinary surgery or training club may be aware of puppies for sale in your area and will know the best breeders. They sometimes help to find suitable homes for dogs or will put you in contact with the kennels in your region. If you know people who own the breed you like, or see them exercising their dogs when you are out walking, don't be afraid to ask them about the breed and where they got their dog – personal recommendations are useful. Avoid advertisements that offer a large selection of breeds for sale.

Dog shows are a good place to look at different breeds and talk to the breeders. You can find out if any litters of puppies are going to be available soon locally.

Dog shows

You can also visit dog shows and training classes
to find out more about the breeds that interest you
and talk to the owners and breeders. This will help
you determine which lines within breeds are good
prospects and which to avoid. Today's All Breed
Championship Shows are held over two or three
days, and you should try to find out in advance on
which day your favourite breed is being exhibited;
a telephone call to The Kennel Club or a glance
through the canine newspapers will reveal which
one. Note that the smaller Open Shows, which take
place over one day, may not schedule your breed,
particularly if it is quite rare, so check this out in
advance to save yourself a wasted journey.

Breed rescue societies

Not everybody wants the problems associated with
owning and socializing a young puppy, and you may
prefer to acquire an adult dog. There is a network of
breed rescue organizations throughout Britain - a

Dog showing can be great fun
and you may become a devotee
yourself in the fullness of time.

must know

There are two main
reasons why a pedigree
dog is a pedigree:
• Its ancestry is known
and recorded.
• It breeds true to type,
so a dog and bitch of
one breed will produce
replicas of themselves
(colour excepted).
By owning a pedigree
dog, you will know the
size to which it will grow
and the temperament it
is likely to develop.

quick search on the internet or a telephone call to The Kennel Club will provide their contact details.

There are many reasons for dogs to be in rescue, including broken marriages, deaths and owners moving abroad. Many of these dogs will come from a happy home, are well trained and can become a fully accepted older dog in any household. However, some will have been ill treated and these dogs will require lots of tender loving care before they have confidence in their new home.

Because of the difficulties, potential owners should be prepared for some searching questions before the dog is handed over to them, so do not be offended if you are asked some personal and pertinent questions, or if a visit is arranged to view your home and garden and assess whether you are a suitable owner. Usually a small fee is involved for 'rescuing' a dog, so that the rescue organization can recover some of their expenses and help support other abandoned dogs in their care. It is unusual for the Kennel Club documents to be made available to new owners; this is to prevent the possibility of further abuse to the dog.

Greyhound rescue

Thousands of racing Greyhounds are bred in Britain and Southern Ireland – far too many for the market to absorb – and, as a result, numerous dogs are abandoned by their owners if they fail to make the grade on the race track. Contrary to some opinions, Greyhounds can be trained easily not to chase small furry animals and they can make very gentle, loving companions. Fortunately, there are specialist rescue organizations for the breed, which not only rehome

Puppies look cute but when they are playing they may get excited, so it's important to be gentle.

ex-racers but actually go to the race tracks in Spain, where many Greyhounds are frequently ill treated, and then buy them back and re-home them either in Britain or elsewhere in Europe.

Puppies love exercise and playing with their owners. Free running and games are the perfect way to bond with your dog and to get to know each other better.

National charities

Some national charities never put down any dog except if it is very old and infirm and, no matter what is done to help it, can never have any quality of life. Both Battersea Dogs' Home and the Dogs Trust give dogs of all breeds, including abandoned mongrels, a chance by re-training them, treating their ailments and matching them very carefully with potential owners. Owners are at liberty to return a dog that fails to fit into its new home, and then further efforts will be made to re-home it, no matter how long it takes. However, if your heart is set on a particular breed, you may have to wait for one to become available.

Selecting the right dog

There is no magic formula for selecting the right dog, whether it's a rescued adult or from a litter of puppies at a breeder's kennels. It is always best if the entire family go together to make a choice; everybody should express their opinion as the dog is going to live in your home with all of you and will become a family member.

This Airedale puppy wants a game, but you must determine the rules and boundaries of acceptable behaviour to prevent problems occurring in later life.

Opposite: Even small toy breeds like this Pomeranian need a lot of care and attention, so only own a dog if you have the time and energy to devote to its care.

Breed rescues

Staff at rescue centres will be concerned that the right dog goes to the right family and they will ask personal questions about your house and garden, whether there will be anybody at home during the day to look after the dog and whether you have other pets. You will be shown dogs that have been carefully assessed and will be told candidly if there are likely to be any problems.

Behaviour problems

There are some disadvantages of getting a dog from a breed rescue. For example, it may have been a stray, lost or abandoned by the previous owners, and nobody will know how much training it has received, any illnessor health problems it may have had or whether it has been abused. The staff will try to detect and correct any behaviour problems, but in the privacy of your own home the dog may lack confidence and be troubled by the unfamiliar surroundings. Thus it may be hard work settling it in and you will need to be patient until it understands what you expect. If you are kind, play with the dog, exercise it and establish a routine, it is remarkable how quickly it will attach itself to you and your family.

Records

The breed rescue should supply you with the dog's veterinary record, so that in the event of illness or accident your vet will know what treatment has been administered. There will also be a record of its vaccinations which you will have to keep up to date.

Breeders

There are several ways of finding a breeder: by personal recommendation, contacting The Kennel Club, training clubs or relevant breed society, or by making contacts at dog shows. Many of the minority breeds have only a few breeders in the country and you may well have to go on a waiting list for a puppy. The choice of breeder is important, so if you distrust one, do not buy a puppy from them.

When you go to the breeder's home to view the puppies, insist on seeing their mother and watch the dogs carefully to see how they all behave together and interact.

They should have taken care to rear the puppies in their home environment and made every effort to maximize their health and socialization. The ideal breeder has a policy of breeding sound dogs, both mentally and physically, and will be interested in the puppy's future home and life.

Genes

Good breeders select suitable parent dogs from genetic lines that not only produce dogs with good temperaments but also minimize inherited defects. From your research, you will know which, if any, genetic abnormalities affect your favourite breeds. One of the most frequent inherited conditions in the larger breeds is hip dysplasia, and the best breeders have been working on this problem for years. They are now succeeding in reducing the incidence in most breeds. You should find out the average score for the breed and ask the breeder of the puppy you

Some puppies, such as this little Yorkshire Terrier, are tiny and must be handled with care.

Lhasa Apsos tend to be healthy with fewer inherited defects than some other breeds. Their heavy coat requires a lot of grooming and it may be easier to cut it short like this.

are thinking of buying to show you the parents'
scores or the mother's British Veterinary Association/
Kennel Club (BVA/KC) score sheet. If it is very much
higher than the norm, you would be well advised not
to buy one of the puppies. There are other genetic
tests available, particularly for eye conditions that
affect some breeds. The Kennel Club will be happy to
advise you on the question of genetic abnormalities
occurring in various breeds.

Viewing the puppies

Take your family to see the puppies, which should
be over eight weeks old, but make sure that any
young children are under control. It is possible that
the puppies may never have encountered children
before and will become disturbed, over-excited or
even frightened. Always ask to see the puppies'
mother, so that you can ensure they really are her
offspring, get an accurate idea of the fully-grown
size of an adult dog and, more importantly, make
a quick assessment of her temperament. If the
breeder is reluctant to let you view the mother
or refuses to do so, you are right to be suspicious
and you should walk away and look elsewhere.

**These Yorkies look so appealing
that it is easy to want to take
them all home with you! Don't
be swayed by their cuteness, but
let your reason predominate.**

Which puppy?

Whichever sex you have decided upon, ask the breeder to remove the others and then examine the puppies individually. Look for any sort of discharge from the eyes, the mouth, the anus or the vulva; if any is present, don't take that puppy. The runt of the litter should also be discounted, no matter how appealing. Never be persuaded to buy a puppy at a lower price because 'there is something minor wrong with it'. Therein lies trouble. If the breeder persists in trying to persuade you, walk away.

However, if everything looks good, then watch the puppies closely and observe their behaviour. If you want a bold and confident puppy, which is full of character, look for the most extrovert one, which approaches you with a mixture of curiosity and happiness. However, if you want a more reserved dog with a gentle character, then select a more cautious puppy who is a little apprehensive initially but then comes to you and interacts with you.

It's difficult to choose the right dog for you when presented with several puppies who all look very similar. Observe them and look out for the sociable, adventurous, gentle and shy pups in a litter.

Temperament

The breed you end up with will depend, to some extent, on your character and temperament, and it is important to match the right owner with the right dog. Ultimately, selecting the characteristics in a breed that will best suit and complement your requirements is the key to a long and happy partnership between owner and dog.

Socialization

Sociable, outgoing owners need friendly dogs who enjoy human company and are not nervous, shy or aggressive. Some genetic lines and breeds predispose puppies to be sociable and confident, and these breeds will make better family pets. Socialization is very important and all puppies should be exposed from an early age to a wide range of people, dogs and other animals, noises, experiences and situations. This process starts with the mother and littermates in the breeder's home and continues with the new owner. Good socialization will help a puppy to develop and grow into a contented, friendly dog who will be a pleasure to own.

must know

A responsible breeder will breed from healthy dogs without genetic defects and with good temperaments. The mother and her puppies will be kept in a healthy household environment where they can be socialized to everyday events. Puppies will be encouraged to toilet away from the nest area and will play with toys.

Sociable dogs for families

If you want a good-natured dog who will fit into a family, possibly with young children and a busy lifestyle, you could consider one of the gundog breeds. They tend to be loyal, relatively easy to train, exceedingly biddable, placid and anxious to please their owners. Suitable breeds include:

- Cocker Spaniel
- Golden Retriever
- Pointer
- Labrador Retriever

Independent dogs for families

Some breeds have quite a strong character and an independent streak, making them more suitable pets for families with older teenage children. If you are strong willed and want an active dog who will interact well with the family as well as friends and visitors, you might consider the following breeds. They all require kind but firm handling.

- Airedale
- Beagle
- German Shepherd Dog
- Staffordshire Bull Terrier
- Small terriers with strong natures, e.g. the West Highland White Terrier and Jack Russell Terrier

Staffies have a reputation for being tough, energetic dogs. It is very important with such breeds to train and socialize the puppies with other dogs and people.

Boxers are the jokers and juvenile delinquents of the canine world. They are full of energy and need a lot of their owners' time.

Even as puppies, Springers are very energetic and will enjoy as much exercise and games in the garden as you can give them.

Energetic dogs for fit owners

Some breeds are very boisterous, energetic and need a lot of exercise, both physically and mentally through playing games with their owners. Many of the working breeds fall into this category, but they demand equally energetic owners. If you like to keep fit, are prepared to walk or run many miles a day and have the time to devote to playing games with your dog, you might like one of the following:

- Border Collie
- Boxer
- Jack Russell Terrier
- Springer Spaniel

Companion dogs for quiet owners

Some people, especially the elderly, don't want the challenge or have the energy for owning a large, strong-willed, competitive dog. They want a mild-natured companion breed which will be tolerant of close contact, forge a strong bond with them, and not require so much exercise. Spirited small breeds with gentle temperaments include the following:

- Bichon Frise
- Cavalier King Charles Spaniel
- Miniature Poodle
- Pomeranian
- Pekingese
- Pug
- Yorkshire Terrier

Taking your puppy home

When you have made up your mind and have chosen a puppy, it is time for business. The registration of dogs and puppies with The Kennel Club is very important as you will not be able to show a dog or breed from it without registration.

Registering your puppy

The cost is normally absorbed by the breeder. At the time of buying you may be dismissive, thinking that you do not need registration, but do not be hasty. You don't know how your interests may change in the future, and many great careers in the world of dogs have started with the purchase of a first puppy. If the papers have not yet been issued by The Kennel Club, you must ask the breeder to state in writing that the documents have been applied for and will be sent in the immediate future. When you receive the registration document, there is a 'Transfer' form on the reverse side. Complete it and return it to The Kennel Club with the appropriate fee and the dog will be transferred into your name.

Buying your puppy

It is a good idea to discuss a 'buy back' agreement with the breeder. Some reputable breeders will agree to have the puppy back if, for any reason, he is not suitable or your home conditions change so much that you cannot look after him. And don't forget to get a signed and dated receipt when you hand over the money. Enquire about insurance – some insurance companies, working in conjunction with breeders, offer four to six weeks' free cover.

must know

Be prepared and get ready in advance for the arrival of your new dog. Stock up on food, bowls, bedding, toys, chews, a suitable collar and lead and other items of essential equipment. Don't leave it to the last minute or until after your new puppy's arrival in your home.

This handsome Dobermann puppy will grow up into a large and powerful adult. It needs firm but kind training and socializing from the earliest possible age.

Opposite: Cocker Spaniels are not so docile as they look. Spirited, fun-loving and playful, they can be very obstinate at times.

This is useful because it encompasses the most vulnerable time in a puppy's life.

The breeder should also give you five or six days' supply of the food they normally feed the puppy, together with a diet sheet. Keeping to the same food for several days will help prevent to stomach upsets as the puppy settles in to its new home. If you want to change its diet, only introduce new foods gradually, observing the puppy carefully to check that there are no adverse effects.

Collecting your puppy

When the time comes to collect your puppy and take him home, be prepared. It may not have been in a car before unless it was to go to the vet for health checks or vaccinations, so have a soft blanket available, sit the pup on someone's lap and stroke it gently and reassuringly. Have a plentiful supply of tissues to hand in case it is car sick. Don't be cross with the puppy if this happens – it doesn't think it is doing anything wrong. Do everything possible to comfort the dog and make it think that travelling in a car is a pleasurable experience.

If you have a long drive home, take a water bottle and small bowl. However, don't let the puppy get out of the car to relieve itself, especially in lay-bys which can be sources of infection.

Settling the puppy in

It is important to plan ahead for the arrival of your new puppy and buy all the equipment and toys it will need before you bring it home. You must also make sure that your garden is securely fenced and escape-proof and that the puppy has a quiet place

Puppies need plenty of toys and suitable chews to keep them busy and occupied.

There is no easy alternative to toilet training. Take your dog outside regularly, whatever the weather - rain or shine.

to call its own, where it can sleep or rest quietly undisturbed. When the pup arrives in its new home, don't pressurize it – just allow the dog to explore and sniff around quietly and find its own level.

Put a comfortable bed in a draught-free corner with a soft, comfortable blanket or vet bed to lie on. This bed must be inviolable, and once the puppy goes to it for a rest it must not be disturbed. Don't allow children to smother the new arrival with love and get it over-excited initially – a tickle under the chin, a pat on the head and a few soothing words will be sufficient. The pup will let you know when it wants more attention. Be patient, take your time and it will become your faithful companion.

Toilet training

Dogs appreciate routine and your puppy will like to know that it is fed at the same times each day and taken out at the same times. Perhaps your most urgent task with a new puppy is to housetrain it, and this will involve taking the dog outside and

encouraging it to toilet immediately after food, a drink, a boisterous game, awaking from a sleep and before the night's sleep. Don't be tempted to skip this duty just because it's cold or raining outside or there's something on television that you want to watch. It's important to accompany the dog and praise it lavishly when it performs the required action. Your puppy will soon learn what is expected of it and this will make your life easier – and cleaner!

Social interaction and training

Make time to play games with your puppy and interact with it. Provide a variety of interesting toys and chews to keep it busy and prevent boredom setting in. Equally, make sure that it is socialized effectively and exposed to a wide range of different people, children, other animals, household noises and car travel. This will help the puppy to grow up into a well-adjusted, sociable adult dog. Exercise it regularly, but remember that you cannot take it outside your home into public places until it has completed a course of vaccinations.

Once your puppy is old enough to venture out, it is a good idea to take it to local puppy socialization and training classes. It can be a fun evening for both of you and will help the puppy to learn how to communicate and play with other dogs. You can also start domestic obedience training by taking classes of the Good Citizens Scheme and earning bronze, silver and gold medals as you improve. Always be patient, don't punish the pup if it does something wrong and be sure to reward good behaviour with lavish praise and treats. Therein lies the way to a happy partnership between owner and dog.

must know

You can help prevent problem behaviour when your puppy is older by encouraging good manners now. Don't feed titbits at the table, allow it to bark excessively, jump up at people or pull on the lead. When the pup is bigger and stronger, these habits will not seem so endearing.

Hereditary diseases

As in humans, dogs can inherit a wide range of diseases, and these may occur in pedigree and cross-bred animals. They are caused by genetic faults or aberrations in the breeding line.

Young Irish Wolfhounds should not have excessive exercise while they are still growing and their bones are developing.

Genetic faults

The genetic background to many hereditary ailments can be extremely complicated and is of concern to all professional breeders, veterinarians and geneticists. Screening tests are available for tendencies to some hereditary diseases, and potential owners of dogs, particularly pedigrees, should consult their vet about possible inherited health problems within the breed and ask the breeder about the lineage and history of the dams and sires before purchasing a puppy. Although some hereditary diseases are treatable, the underlying genetic faults can only be eliminated by skilful breeding based on genetic science. There is some information overleaf on hereditary diseases and the breeds that are most commonly affected.

Hip dysplasia

This is one of the most common inherited diseases and affects many breeds. In a normal, healthy dog the hip is a 'ball and socket' joint, allowing a wide range of movement. The rounded end at the top of the femur fits tightly into the cup-shaped socket in the pelvis. In hip dysplasia, a shallow socket develops with a distorted femur head and slack joint ligaments. There can be excessive movement between the femur and pelvis, leading to a malfunctioning joint which will gradually become arthritic.

Early symptoms

If a puppy develops severe hip dysplasia it may have difficulty walking. Getting up from a sitting position may be painful and it will cry out. When the pup runs, it may use both hind legs together in a 'bunny hop' or look as though it's swaying. These symptoms may be identifiable from five months onwards. Mildly affected puppies may show no signs at all of hip dysplasia at this age, but they will begin to develop arthritis at about eight years of age.

Hip dysplasia scheme

The British Veterinary Association and the Kennel Club run a joint scheme (the BVA/KC hip dysplasia scheme) based on hip scoring. The vet submits the X-ray, bearing the KC registration number of the

must know

Hip dysplasia affects some dog breeds more than others, especially German Shepherd Dogs, Labradors, Retrievers and Rottweilers. It is also becoming more common in smaller breeds but seldom affects mongrels.

Labradors and Retrievers are both susceptible to hip dysplasia.

Common hereditary diseases

Disease name	Nature of disease	Breeds most commonly affected
Bones/skeleton		
Hip dysplasia	Deformation of hip joint	Labrador, other Retrievers, German Shepherd
Elbow dysplasia	Deformation of elbow joint	German Shepherd, Afghan Hound
Osteochondrosis dessicans	Disease of joint surfaces, particularly shoulder	Larger breeds, including Border Collie, Golden Retriever, Great Dane, Labrador Retriever
Wobbler syndrome	Malformation of neck bones	Great Dane, Dobermann
Eyes		
Entropion	Inturned eyelids	Many breeds but particularly Shar Pei
Ectropion	Out-turned eyelids	Clumber Spaniel, St Bernard
Cherry eye	Enlargement of gland in third eyelid	American Cocker Spaniel
Progressive retinal atrophy (PRA)	Degeneration of retina with progressive loss of sight	Irish Setter, Springer Spaniel
Collie eye	Another degeneration of the retina	Collie, Shetland Sheepdog
Glaucoma	Increased pressure within the eye	American Cocker Spaniel, Poodle
Cataract	Cloudiness of lens in the eye	Poodle, Labrador Retriever, Golden Retriever, American Cocker Spaniel, Beagle
Cardiovascular		
Subaortic stenosis	Narrowing of the aorta with effects on heart	Boxer, German Shepherd, German Shorthaired Pointer, Newfoundland
Pulmonic stenosis	Narrowing of pulmonary artery with effects on heart	Beagle
Ventricular septal	Heart defect	Bulldog 'hole in the heart' defect
Patent ductus arteriosus	Heart defect	Poodle, German Shepherd, Collie, Shetland Sheepdog, Pomeranian
Blood disorders		
Haemophilia	Clotting defects	Many breeds
Von Willebrand's	A special form of haemophilia	Golden Retriever, German Shepherd, Dobermann and Scottie
Neurological		
Cerebellar atrophy	Degeneration of the cerebellum in brain	Many breeds, including Rough Collie, Kerry Blue, Gordon Setter
Deafness		Border Collie, Boston Terrier, Bull Terrier, Collie, Dalmatian, English Setter, Old English Sheepdog
Hydrocephalus ('water on the brain') and epilepsy		Both can occur in many breeds and they are suspected of having a genetic cause
Hormonal		
Hypothyroidism	Underactive thyroid gland	Beagle, Dobermann, Golden Retriever
Cushing's Disease	Overactive adrenal glands	Poodle

Some breed lines of Irish Setters
are affected by the eye disease
progressive retinal atrophy (PRA).

dog, to the scheme. Each hip is then scored from
0 to 54, making a total of 108 maximum between
the two hips. The lower the score the better, and
0:0 is the best score possible.

You should not breed from any dog or bitch which
has a higher hip score than the average for the breed
or hip dysplasia will never be reduced or eliminated
from that breed. When buying a puppy, always check
that both its parents have been X-rayed, scored, and
have achieved a low score. This does not guarantee
that the puppy will not develop hip dysplasia but it
does help to reduce the chances.

Treatment

If mild hip dysplasia is treated in a growing puppy
with anabolic steroids, limited exercise and diet,
it will often grow into a healthy adult dog. However,
you may have to restrict the amount of exercise
later on, too. In severe cases, surgery is available.

want to know more?

• For more information
on which dog breed is
right for you, and to
source a responsible
breeder, check out The
Kennel Club website:
www.the-kennel-club.
org.uk
• To learn about the
Good Citizens Scheme,
look at The Kennel Club
website (see above)
• For more details of all
the breeds, see *Breed
Standards*, published by
The Kennel Club and
available from them
• *Dogs Today* magazine
is a useful source of
information: www.dogs
todaymagazine.co.uk

2 Hounds

This group of dogs falls into two categories: hounds that hunt by scent and those that hunt by sight. The sight hounds are possibly among the oldest breeds of dog; most of them originated in Persia, Arabia and south-west Asia. These lean, running dogs were bred for speed to outrun their prey and include the Afghan Hound, Greyhound and Irish Wolfhound. In contrast, the scent hounds use their sensitive nose and great endurance to track and hunt down game. Within this group are the Beagle, Basset Hound and Bloodhound. Scent hounds enjoy living together in packs, whether it's a pack of hunting hounds or a family pack.

Afghan Hound

One of the great sights in the canine world is an Afghan Hound running at speed; its smooth action surrounded by a moving cloud of silken hair has to be seen to be believed. This great sight hound is one of the most glamorous of all the dog breeds.

must know

Strangers ✓✓✓✓
Aloof, suspicious, will warn

Temperament ✓✓✓✓
Happy, playful

Exercise ✓✓✓✓✓
Plenty

Grooming ✓✓✓✓
Three times a week

Other dogs ✓✓✓
Agreeable

Summary
Independent, intelligent and affectionate

History

Like so many ancient breeds, the origins of the Afghan Hound are a matter of guesswork and conjecture. Some canophilists believe that they lie in ancient Egypt, but most think they came from the remote mountain areas of Afghanistan circa 2,000BC. Afghan Hounds hunt by sight, and were developed to hunt deer, gazelles, wolves and snow leopards. They were also farmers' guard dogs, ensuring the security of sheep and cattle.

Afghan Hounds were virtually unheard of in Britain until the 1890s when they were brought home by soldiers fighting on the frontier of India and Afghanistan. They more or less disappeared until the 1920s when interest in the breed revived and they became popular show dogs.

Temperament

Paradoxically, this breed appears aloof and arrogant but, if properly trained and socialized, they are very happy, playful dogs. Being pack dogs, they do not like being left alone, and if this happens they can be destructive. They are delightful with children, although care should be exercised around toddlers. Inside the home, they are quiet, but outside they are the very demons of action.

Appearance

Perhaps the most elegant of all the hounds, the Afghan has a profuse silky coat, which can be in any colour. When standing, Afghans exhibit a long neck with a proud carriage of the head. The tail has a ring at the end. Male dogs are 68–74cm (27–29in) tall, whereas bitches are 63–69cm (25–27in).

General care

The coat is the Afghan Hound's crowning glory, but to maintain it in good condition and prevent tangles it needs combing at least three times a week and bathing with a special canine shampoo every month because it picks up dirt when exercising outside. Being natural athletes, these dogs need to be fed highly-nutritious food in the correct amounts as well as plenty of exercise. Ideally, they love to be with their owners inside the home.

must know

There are some rare genetic anomalies in this breed, so potential buyers should always check these out with recognized breeders and The Kennel Club.

The Afghan Hound's long, silky coat needs regular grooming to keep it free of tangles.

Basset Hound

It would take a hard-hearted person to resist the beguiling eyes of a Basset Hound. A long-bodied, long-eared, short-legged scent hound, this affectionate and placid-natured dog is equally happy in either a domestic or hunting environment.

must know

Strangers ✓✓✓
Not unfriendly

Temperament ✓✓✓✓
Friendly, playful

Exercise ✓✓✓✓✓
Plenty including walks and free running

Grooming ✓
Only once a week

Other dogs ✓✓✓
Generally friendly

Summary
Benign but a bit lazy, needs stimulation

History

The Basset breeds originated in France and were mentioned in canine books as early as 1585. The short-legged Basset was a result of inbreeding dwarf hounds. Imported into England in 1866 by Lord Galway, it was developed further by the artist Sir Everett Millais who added Bloodhound to the mix, creating an exceptional scent hound which was capable of penetrating the thickest cover yet slow enough for hunters to follow on foot.

Temperament

This is an excellent pet dog, fond of children, benign and friendly. However, it tends to be a little lazy unless it is stimulated by people to play games, go out for a walk or go hunting. Being pack dogs, Basset Hounds do not like to be left alone; their natural place is with their family (human) or at least with a canine companion. Like many other hounds, they are not the easiest breed to train, and only those owners who recognize the need for sensitive understanding will be successful. If you are thinking of owning one of these handsome dogs, make sure that your garden is escape proof, as once a Basset makes up his mind to go hunting he is oblivious to everything else.

Appearance

This middle-weight hound (about 55lb) has a long body with short muscular legs. Like a Bloodhound, it has some loose head skin with long ears. The tail (stern) is carried vertically with a sabre curve when moving. Any hound colour is recognized. The ideal height is 33–38cm (13–15in) at the withers.

General care

The Basset's easy-care coat only needs combing and rubbing over with a hound glove once a week. The ears need special attention, as they must be kept clean, dry and free from parasites. The breed can be greedy, so take care that your dog does not run to fat. Remember he is a hunting breed, has enormous stamina and needs to be active; plenty of exercise is vitally important for adult dogs. Hunting is now banned in the UK but even a pet benefits by being kept in hard hunting condition. Puppies up to 10–12 months should not be over-exercised and should avoid stairs and steep climbs.

must know

There some genetic anomalies to guard against: entropion, eye gonioscopy, paneosteitis (transitory lameness), some back problems (due to length) elbow dysplasia and skin problems. Always consult the breeder.

Bassetts are very appealing and handsome dogs but they need a lot of exercise to stay really fit.

Beagle

A small hound dating from Norman times, the Beagle evolved from the Talbot and Southern Hounds. A further mix with small hounds produced the breed that was first recorded in the 'Privy Accounts' of Henry VIII. As larger hunted animals became more scarce, the Beagle was bred to hunt hares.

must know

Beagles are hardy, long-lived companion dogs although, rarely, they may suffer hip problems. An eye problem is also under investigation.

Temperament

The intelligent Beagle can adjust well to town or country life. It readily accepts children and it likes to feel part of the human pack. Beagles are happy, easy-going and very people-orientated, adapting well to most environments. However, they are not the easiest dogs to train and require a lot of kindness and patience.

This Beagle has the conformation and coat colour of the traditional English type of hound.

Appearance

Small to medium in size, two varieties of Beagles exist in America, one not exceeding 33cm (13in) in height, while the other is taller but does not exceed 38cm (15in). In Great Britain, 33–40cm (13–16in) is acceptable. Tri-colours are most popular with a black back, tan sides and top of legs, and a white chest, stomach and lower legs.

The markings and build of this Beagle are favoured in the United States.

Work

As a pack dog, the Beagle has few equals. It is not quarrelsome and it is relatively easy to train for hunting. Having short legs, it works slower than the Harrier or English Hound but hunts cheerfully with its flag (tail) held high. Beagle packs are usually hunted with huntsmen on foot.

General care

Beagles need plenty of exercise, which must be augmented with play in the garden. They eat well and care should be taken to keep them in athletic form as they have a tendency to be overweight. A weekly brush and a polish with a chamois leather keeps them looking good.

must know

Strangers ✓✓✓✓
Will warn but no aggression

Temperament ✓✓✓✓✓
Easy-going, friendly

Exercise ✓✓✓✓✓
Plenty

Grooming ✓
Weekly brush and polish

Other dogs ✓✓✓
No problems

Summary
A happy, laid-back companion

Bloodhound

If any breed has a claim to be part of the British heritage, it is the noble Bloodhound. The traditional adage that 'the Bloodhound is the father of all hounds' gives us a clue as to its importance as a breed. Powerful and dignified, this affectionate dog is a sensitive, loyal and affectionate companion.

must know

Strangers ✓✓✓
Friendly; not a good guard dog

Temperament ✓✓✓✓
Happy, playful

Exercise ✓✓✓✓✓
Lots, including free running

Grooming ✓
Minimal: once a week

Other dogs ✓✓✓✓
No problems

Summary
Lovely gentle nature but needs space

History

In the fifth century AD, the monks of Hubert's Abbey in the Ardennes, Belgium, bred the black and tan St Hubert's Hound which was brought to Britain by William the Conqueror and named the Bloodhound. Men hunted deer with bows and arrows, and the Bloodhound, with its incredible scenting ability, was able to follow the blood trail, bringing the hunters in for the kill. As the number of deer diminished, lifestyles changed and foxes were hunted for 'sport', the Bloodhound was dropped in favour of the faster Foxhound. The noble Bloodhound was relegated to tracking poachers, escaped criminals, lost old people and children. Its reputation was re-established in 1897 with the new Association of Bloodhound Breeders who set up a series of tracking tests.

Temperament

The original 'laid back' hound, the Bloodhound is likely to lick a burglar to death when it catches him. Being a pack hound, it loves its family and that includes tolerating boisterous children. Although sometimes reserved, the Bloodhound hates being left alone. Treat this dog kindly and it will reward you with both affection and great companionship.

Appearance

The Bloodhound is a big, loose-skinned hound with a smooth, short coat in black and tan, liver and tan or red, with long, low-set ears.

General care

Plenty of exercise, including some free running, is essential for this breed, but take care as once its nose goes down on a scent it will be gone, deaf to all your entreaties. Grooming needs are minimal – once a week, give your dog a good brush, cleaning the ears and skin wrinkles. Good-quality food, fed in adequate quantities, is paramount to develop and maintain quality bone structure.

must know

Entropion and joint problems can affect this breed, but responsible breeders are controlling these aspects. Some dogs are prone to bloat, so take the breeder's advice on diet.

The majestic Bloodhound looks formidable but is actually a big softie and loves its family 'pack'.

Dachshund

Mystery veils the real origins of this alert, lively breed. Its German name is *Teckel*, a word found at the base of an ancient Egyptian sculpture of familiarly long-bodied, short-legged dogs. The word 'Dachshund' means 'badger dog', and it is one of the oldest hunting dog breeds in Germany today.

must know

All varieties can have back problems and they should not be allowed to run up and down steps or stairs. Only buy Miniatures from eye-tested parents.

Breed varieties

The different sizes and coats have evolved since around 1850 and today the most popular variety is the Miniature Long-haired Dachshund. Very few, if any, Dachshunds hunt in Britain but they have not lost their natural instincts – a few are still used in Germany and France. They will go underground but are in danger of being trapped. At one time, the Standards hunted foxes, deer and even boar.

Temperament

The Dachshund is very affectionate within its family. Playful and mischievous, it is sometimes stubborn as befits a hunting dog. An adaptable breed, it lives with equal ease in the town or countryside. Intelligent and easily trained, it is sometimes spirited, always humourous. The Long-haireds are more independent than the Wires and Smooths, which make more demonstrative family pets.

The Smooth-haired Dachshund makes a spirited companion and good family pet.

Despite its size, the Dachshund is a game little dog that loves hunting.

General care

All varieties adore activity and need daily free running and play. Each variety also has its miniature equivalent. Whereas Smooths need a soft brush and polish weekly, the Long-haireds need brushing and combing bi-weekly, and Wire-haireds should be hand stripped every three months.

Appearance

This long, low dog is sometimes known as the 'sausage dog'. All colours are acceptable but only small white patches on the chest are permitted. Standards should weigh 9–12kg (20–26lb) whereas miniatures should not exceed 5kg (11lb).

The Dachshund has a long, tapering head with medium almond-shaped eyes and high-set ears.

Norwegian Elkhound

The Elkhound is one of the oldest known domesticated canines, and skeletons of a very similar breed of dog, which have been excavated in Norway, are over 6,000 years old. Originally, the Elkhound, with its acute senses, was an all-purpose farm guard dog, which was also used for hunting Elk.

must know

Strangers ✓✓✓
Friendly until proved otherwise

Temperament ✓✓✓✓
Friendly, playful

Exercise ✓✓✓✓✓
Plenty including walks and free running

Grooming ✓
Only once a week

Other dogs ✓✓✓
Relaxed unless challenged

Summary
Easy personality with a streak of individuality

Work

The Elkhound can scent an Elk up to three miles away. It possesses an extraordinary stamina and will pursue its prey over incredible distances on the worst possible terrain. This dog has also hunted bears and wolves successfully. Today, with hunting under strict control, the Elkhound has become a popular pet and show dog.

Temperament

The Norwegian Elkhound should be trained and socialized from a puppy with kindness and patience. Elkhounds are hunters by nature and they can be boisterous, but they are also faithful and affectionate. Generally good with children, they should be kept away from babies and toddlers in case of accidents. When a dog wishes to sleep, it should always be left in peace. Indifferent to weather conditions, it loves to be outside in the snow.

Appearance

The Elkhound is of medium size – dogs are 52cm (20.5in) in height and weigh 23kg (51lb) whereas bitches are 49cm (19.5in) and 20kg (44lb). A Spitz breed, it is easily recognized by the pricked ears facing forward, the distinctive tail curled over the back and the grey, thick, cold-proof coat.

General care

The Elkhound is not a fussy eater and, being a hunting breed, it should be kept in a fit, athletic condition, so even in a domestic environment it will need plenty of exercise every day. In fact, it is almost impossible to exhaust an Elkhound. The coat must be deep combed and brushed once or twice a week; not to do so causes tangles and mats which are an ideal breeding ground for parasites and can be acutely uncomfortable for the dog. These dogs moult twice a year, and during this time daily grooming will be required.

must know

Some PRA and hip dysplasia are present in this breed. Only buy an Elkhound from breeders who have had the appropriate veterinary tests carried out.

The Elkhound is one of the oldest breeds. Note the characteristic curled tail carried over the back.

Greyhound

Hunting dogs were probably the first canines to be domesticated and developed by man because they helped provide him with food. Greyhounds have always been appreciated for their speed and cunning. Indeed, they are the world's fastest dogs, running at speeds in excess of 64kph (40mph).

must know

Strangers ✓✓✓
Will warn but no aggression

Temperament ✓✓✓✓
Friendly, playful

Exercise ✓✓✓✓✓
Plenty including walks and free running

Grooming ✓
Only once a week

Other dogs ✓✓✓
Be careful with very small dogs

Summary
Good all-round family pet

History

Although very little is known of the origins of the Greyhound, its efficacy and grace were admired as far back as King Solomon. Images of them have been depicted in stone-age caves, as decoration on ancient Greek vases and in Egyptian pyramids. Through eons of time, this breed was the favourite of royalty. Known in Britain since before 800AD, killing a Greyhound in the time of Hywel of Wales meant death to the perpetrator.

As hunting habits changed, the Greyhound was only used for coursing hare (now illegal). However, in 1926, the first Greyhound Stadium was opened in Manchester, England, and racing soon became a popular sport, although it is declining now.

Temperament

Greyhounds are gentle and affectionate dogs. Intelligent and easygoing by nature, they are easily trained and take up very little room in the home, despite their size. However, they are genetically programmed to chase small animals, like dogs and cats, so every endeavour must be made to prevent this, especially if you adopt a dog that has retired from the race track.

Appearance

Strongly built, muscular dogs, Greyhounds come in a range of different coat colours. The ideal height for dogs is 71-76cm (28-30in); bitches are slightly smaller at 68-71cm (27-28in).

General care

Being the ultimate canine athlete, the Greyhound needs plenty of exercise, including free running, and should be fed the correct amount of nourishing food. Their coats are fine and short and are 'easy care'; they need brushing only once a week, followed by a smoothing with a hound glove.

must know

Breeders of Greyhounds report no serious health faults within the breed. This is generally a very healthy dog to own.

Lean, lithe and very muscular, the Greyhound is built for speed and is the world's fastest dog.

Irish Wolfhound

Like most big sight hounds, the origins of this majestic dog are steeped in myth and mystery. There is little doubt, however, that the Irish Wolfhound stems from the hounds of ancient Egypt and arrived in Ireland circa 300–500BC with marauding Celtic tribes who had acquired them from Phoenician traders.

must know

Strangers ✓✓✓
Will warn but affable

Temperament ✓✓✓✓
Laid back, affectionate

Exercise ✓✓✓✓✓
Adult dogs need plenty

Grooming ✓
Minimal: once a week

Other dogs ✓✓✓
Accepts all friendly breeds

Summary
Gentle, loyal with a liking for quiet children

History

In Ireland, the early hounds were bred with large, indigenous, hairy dogs to produce a big dog that was impervious to bad weather and able to tackle wolves and boar. So successful were they that they rid Ireland of these two species by around 1770, but without their work, Irish Wolfhounds themselves became virtually extinct. One man, Captain George Graham, set about recreating the breed from about 1865 onwards, using, it is believed, Great Danes, Scottish Deerhounds, Russian Wolfhounds, Pyrenean Sheepdogs and Tibetan Mastiffs.

Temperament

These gentle giants are extremely affectionate, quiet and laid back but fierce in action. They are playful and good with children whom they allow to take liberties. However, babies and toddlers should not be left alone with them in case of accidents due to their great size. Irish Wolfhounds make loyal companions but they do need early socialization and are fairly difficult to train due to their obstinate hunting dog mentality. Nobody should consider owning one unless they have a spacious home and garden, ideally in the countryside.

Appearance

Irish Wolfhounds are graceful yet muscular with a shaggy, harsh topcoat and an undercoat. Adults should sport long hair over the eyes and a beard. The minimum height for dogs is 79cm (31in); 71cm (28in) for bitches. The minimum weight for dogs is 54.5kg (120lb) while bitches are 40.9kg (90lb).

General care

These dogs crave company; they do not like being left alone. A weekly brush and combing suffices to keep the coat in good condition. They must be fed highly nutritious food when young because of their speedy growth. Not much exercise is required for young dogs until the bones have ossified.

The Irish Wolfhound is the tallest breed. It loves human company and may develop behaviour problems if left for long periods.

must know

Wolfhounds can suffer liver shunt, bone cancer, osteochrondrosis and cardiomyelopathy, none of which are proven hereditary conditions. Check status of hips and eyes with the breeder.

Rhodesian Ridgeback

South Africa is a country of extremes, requiring a special hound to hunt its indigenous animals. The Rhodesian Ridgeback is a rare example of the marriage of European canine breeds with a semi-wild African dog: 'the dog with a snake on its back'.

must know

Strangers ✓✓✓✓✓
Suspicious, will guard family and property

Temperament ✓✓✓✓
Laid back, affectionate

Exercise ✓✓✓✓✓
Will take all you can give

Grooming ✓
Minimal: once a week

Other dogs ✓✓✓
Tolerant but will not be bullied

Summary
Can be wilful but with early socialization is a faithful companion

History

The first European settlers in South Africa bred their Greyhounds, Pointers, Staghounds, Great Danes and Foxhounds with native Hottentot dogs with a striking ridge of hair growing in the reverse direction along the spine. They created a fearless hound of great stamina, combining the hunting instincts of European hounds with the South African hound's capability of holding lions at bay. Their unique qualities were recognized by Cornelius van Rooyen who popularized them in Rhodesia (now Zimbabwe).

Temperament

These dogs require patient, kindly training from an early age; fearless hunters, they can be stubborn and given to individualism. When walking in the country, they should be kept under strict control if there are domestic animals around. Properly trained and socialized, they make a splendid family pet.

Appearance

The Rhodesian Ridgeback is a big, solid dog in various shades of tan. The ridge on the back formed by a line of hair growing in the opposite direction is the escutcheon of the breed. It consists of two identical crowns on either side of the spine at the shoulders, continuing down to the haunch. It should be about 5cm (2in) wide at the crowns, diminishing to a point. The minimum height for dogs is 63–67cm (25–27in); 61–66cm (24–26in) for bitches.

General care

The easy-care coat requires only a weekly brush and comb to remove dead hairs. Ridgebacks are not good city dogs – they need space and cannot get enough exercise, however much you provide. They are indifferent to weather but like to lie in the sun. Although they will live outside in a kennel, they enjoy human company. Food should be monitored carefully, so the dog does not get fat.

must know

Check with the breeder for instances of hip dysplasia and lack of or deformation of the characteristic ridge.

Rhodesian Ridgebacks are large, handsome dogs with a ridge of hair along the length of the back.

Whippet

Since antiquity, man has been breeding small hunting hounds capable of catching small animals for the pot. Whippets have been in Britain since before Roman times, probably bred from small versions of Greyhounds brought by the Celts circa 500BC.

History

Whippets were popular with aristocratic ladies as lap dogs and with working people for their prowess as hunters, providing rabbits for food. During the Industrial Revolution, they were used in England by the Durham and Newcastle miners to indulge their passion for gambling on racing and the rat-pit. Other dog breeds, such as Manchester Terriers, Bedlington Terriers and Italian Greyhounds, were introduced to improve performance. The Whippet, once successful for coursing rabbits and hares (now illegal), is kept now largely as a pet and show dog.

Temperament

This small hunting hound is in its own class: it is one of the fastest dogs in pursuit – up to 65kmph (40 mph) – and can turn in its own length. As a pet dog, however, it is gentle, quiet and sensitive, very affectionate to its human family, especially children.

Appearance

The Whippet resembles a Greyhound except it is smaller, more delicate and elegant. The short coat is very fine and comes in many colours and mixtures. Dogs are 47–51cm (18.5–20in) high, whereas bitches are smaller: 44–47cm (17.5–18.5in).

General care

Grooming is minimal for the Whippet; all these dogs need is a weekly polish with a hound glove. Plenty of exercise is of paramount importance, however, as Whippets need at least two formal walks a day plus free running and play in a garden to keep their brain and body active. They particularly enjoy being active, especially pursuits such as lure coursing, Flyball and Agility. Due to their thin skin and fine coat, they suffer from the cold and wet, so it is a kindness to let them wear a coat in bad weather. As with all running dogs, care should be taken to keep them slim. They are not kennel dogs and like to be in the home watching all the activities.

must know

There are hereditary defects but they are unusual and breeders are working to eliminate them. These include some eye problems and a few skin disorders. Undescended testicles are present in a few lines.

Whippets like nothing better than to be free to run across wide open spaces. Their aerodynamic shaped bodies are designed for fast movement and racing.

want to know more?

• For further details of each hound's appearance and temperament, see *Breed Standards*, which is published in the UK by The Kennel Club
• All the hound breeds have their own breed societies and you can Google them on the Internet. Email their secretaries for details of imminent litters

3 Gundogs

The gundog breeds are now not only reliable working dogs but also some of the world's most popular pet dogs, especially spaniels and Labrador Retrievers. They were developed to work with hunters armed with guns and are divided into five categories: water dogs, pointers, setters, flushing dogs and retrievers. Some breeds, such as the Hunt, Point and Retrieve (HPR) dogs, combine more than one of these qualities, and include the German Shorthaired Pointer and Weimaraner. Gundogs are intelligent, biddable, easy to train and make good companions and family pets.

Labrador Retriever

Worldwide, this is the most popular retriever of all. Almost the perfect gundog, the Labrador Retriever is extremely biddable and has a natural inclination to retrieve on land and water, together with a desire to please and the ability to learn easily. This good-tempered, affectionate dog makes an ideal family pet.

must know

Hip dysplasia is present in some lines as are some eye conditions (TRD, GPRA, CPRA, HC). The best breeders test their dogs. Before you buy a Lab puppy, check with the breeder and ask for the test results.

History

The seventeenth century witnessed considerable trade between Britain and Newfoundland – slates out and salt fish back. The Newfoundlanders had an all-purpose water dog which helped the fishermen to retrieve dropped articles, haul carts and retrieve game. Called St John's Dogs, they were brought to Poole in England by sailors. The Earl of Malmesbury, recognizing their retrieving skills, subsequently developed them as gundogs.

Temperament

An affable and intelligent breed, the Labrador Retriever is tolerant and easy-going both with other dogs and with human beings. A devoted and loyal companion, it enjoys the company of children and will allow them to take liberties. It wants to please its human owners and responds well to kindness, making it an easy dog to train. However, it is easily upset by shouting or harsh treatment.

Opposite: Alert and intelligent, Labrador Retrievers are extremely biddable and easy to train. As well as being excellent gundogs, some work as guide dogs, hearing dogs and even sniffer dogs.

Appearance

A strongly built dog, the Labrador has a broad, deep chest, a distinctive tapering tail and a distinctive short, dense coat which can withstand the cold and

wet. The coat colour may be black, yellow, liver or chocolate. The ideal height for dogs is 56–57cm (22–23in) and slightly less for bitches.

Working Labradors learn to work with their owner as part of the human pack. Even pet Labs love retrieving toys and other objects.

General care
Labrador puppies are very ebullient but, with early and kind domestic training, they will soon fit into

family life. They have a need for love, attention and understanding. Labradors have a voracious appetite and a tendency to overweight, so you must monitor your dog's diet carefully. Stimulating their brains prevents destructive habits forming: owners should invent search and retrieve games and involve them in all family activities. The Labrador is an active, country dog which needs plenty of exercise, free running and play, so don't consider owning this breed unless you have boundless energy as well as lots of space and spare time. Grooming is minimal; just clean the ears and brush the coat once a week to rid it of dead hairs.

must know

Strangers ✓✓✓
Will warn but friendly

Temperament ✓✓✓
Cool and laid back

Exercise ✓✓✓
As much as possible

Grooming ✓
Negligible

Other dogs ✓✓✓✓✓
No problems

Summary ✓✓✓✓✓
A wonderful companion dog and working dog

Labrador puppies look small and cute but they grow up into large, powerful dogs which need a lot of exercise.

Golden Retriever

These excellent retrievers have a soft mouth and good nose for finding lost game. They are easily trained to become all-purpose gundogs and work with enthusiasm, braving the thickest cover and coldest water. Their versatility and intelligence also make them great guide dogs for the blind and assistance dogs for the disabled.

must know

Unfortunately, these retrievers can suffer from hip dysplasia, elbow dysplasia and some eye problems. So only buy from tested stock and check with the breeder in advance.

History

In 1825, Lord Tweedmouth mated his 'Yellow' Retriever to a Tweed Water Spaniel (now extinct). One of the resulting progeny was mated to another Tweed Water Spaniel, the progeny of which was mated back again. It is rumoured that a Bloodhound was added, together with a Sheepdog from a troupe of performing Russian circus dogs, with which his Lordship became enamoured and bought. And thus today's Golden Retriever evolved.

Temperament

This is a gentle, biddable dog, which is highly intelligent and capable of combining the best working qualities with those of a near perfect pet. Delightful family dogs, Golden Retrievers are happy to become a working gundog for the father, an elegant companion and an affectionate playmate.

Appearance

A medium-sized dog, the Golden Retriever is strongly built and muscular with a gentle, loving expression in the eyes. The coat is dense with good feathering and a water-resistant undercoat. The colour varies from a cream to a rich, lustrous gold.

Dogs are 56–61cm (22–24in) in height, whereas bitches are slightly smaller at 51–56cm (20–22in).

General care

The Golden Retriever needs frequent exercise – at least twice a day with lead walking and free running – and plenty of mental stimulation. The retrieving instinct is strong and these dogs love to carry toys and other items and need an outlet for this instinctive behaviour. Owners should play retrieving games with their dogs, throwing a ball, or hiding their toys and encouraging them to hunt for them. They excel at activities such as Obedience and Flyball, and should be brushed and combed at least twice a week to rid the coat of dead hairs, and dirt and tangles from the feathering.

must know

Strangers ✓✓✓
Will warn of approach but no aggression

Temperament ✓✓✓✓✓
A gentle and kindly disposition

Exercise ✓✓✓✓✓
Can never have enough

Grooming ✓✓
Twice-weekly brush and comb

Other dogs ✓✓✓✓
Friendly

Summary
A great companion

The Golden Retriever is a great family pet and working dog.

Flat Coated Retriever

A friendly, active dog, this breed was bred originally for a specific market, namely the shooting gentry. However, although it is still worked as a gundog, finding and retrieving birds, unmarked to its handler, it is also very popular as a family pet and showdog.

must know

Strangers ✓✓✓
Gives loud warning but friendly thereafter

Temperament ✓✓✓✓✓
Mischievous, loyal, affectionate

Exercise ✓✓✓✓✓
Can never have enough

Grooming ✓✓✓
Three times a week

Other dogs ✓✓✓✓
Friendly

Summary
A great companion

History

The accuracy of guns had so improved by the nineteenth century that shooting sitting birds was considered unsporting and the skill of shooting birds in flight was born. Retrievers of the time only picked up dead sitting birds, so a different type of dog was needed to work all terrains, especially water. The St John's Dog (early Labrador) was mated to Setters and large Spaniels to produce a prototype. It dropped out of favour and was superseded by the Labrador after World War I, nearly becoming extinct, but because of its inherent beauty, enthusiasts rescued it and now it is undergoing a revival.

Temperament

This dog is the eternal puppy, full of mischief and humour. Very affectionate, it is good with children but can be clumsy and hurtful if over-enthusiastic. It needs things to do, especially work, Obedience, Agility and long walks. It learns quickly but can forget everything it knows if it is distracted.

Appearance

This is an elegant dog, racy looking but intelligent, with a flat black or liver coat. Its friendliness is demonstrated by an excessively wagging tail. Dogs are 59-61cm (23-24in) in height, while bitches are 56.5-59cm (22-23in). The preferred weight for dogs is 27-36kg (60-80lb); bitches 25-32kg (55-70lb).

General care

This dog needs as much exercise and games as possible; its brain and body need stimulation. Good nutritious food is essential to support its exertions but it must not get fat. No strenuous exercise is advised before the age of six months to allow a young dog's bones and joints to set. To prevent tangles, the coat should be brushed and combed three times a week. Train with patience and kindness, as unkindness causes extreme stress.

must know

Some lines have a propensity to cancer. There is evidence of genetic eye anomalies, so buyers should buy only from breeders who utilize KC/BVA eye tests.

The Flat Coated Retriever makes a wonderful family pet as well as an excellent working gundog.

Cocker Spaniel

This spaniel is believed to have originated in pre-fourteenth-century Spain. It evolved through selective breeding from several gundog breeds, depending on the terrain worked and the prey.

must know

Some Cocker breed lines are susceptible to hip dysplasia and kidney problems. Only buy puppies from eye-tested parents and check with the breeder that no genetic anomalies exist in their breed.

Work

A hallmark of this breed is its happiness when working. Indeed, the Cocker's enthusiasm knows no bounds, underlined by its incessant tail wagging. It hurriedly quarters the ground, freezing as it bolts a bird or rabbit, waiting for the shot, and then going after the next. Remembering where the game lies, the Cocker Spaniel can easily find and retrieve it unmarked because of its extraordinarily soft mouth. Indeed, many dogs can carry eggs around in their mouth without breaking them!

Temperament

Today there are more family pets than there are workers because Cockers are gentle, intelligent, biddable and easily trained. This merry little dog makes the classic companion, mainly because it loves the fellowship of its human family. The Cocker's greatest pleasure is to join in all the family activities, lying by the fire, indulging in horse-play with the children and running in the park as well as going out shooting.

Cockers have long, pendulous ears which can become dirty and matted when feeding.

Opposite: Friendly and fun-loving, the Cocker Spaniel is an ideal family pet.

must know

Strangers ✓✓
Will warn of intruders

Temperament ✓✓✓✓✓
Sweet natured and
co-operative

Exercise ✓✓✓✓
As much as you can

Grooming ✓✓✓✓
Daily attention to ears
and feathering

Other dogs ✓✓✓✓✓
Friendly and sociable

Summary
Happy-go-lucky, makes
a lovely family pet

Appearance

A square, compact dog with an affectionate nature and a soft expression, the Cocker Spaniel is well-muscled with good bone, and an easy mover. It has a silky, flat coat, well-feathered forelegs, underparts and above the hocks. A wide range of colours is acceptable – probably more than in any other breed – but in solid colours (black, red, golden and liver) no white is permitted except on the dog's chest. Dogs may also be particolour, tricolour or black and tan, some with attractive orange eye spots.

Cockers have long, pendulous ears which are set low on the side of the head – so low, in fact, that they have a tendency to fall into the dog's food bowl. Dogs are 39–41cm (15^1/$_2$–16in) in height, while bitches are 38–39cm (15–15^1/$_2$in).

A Cocker Spaniel needs regular grooming to keep its coat in good condition and free from knots. If you start from an early age, both you and your dog will enjoy these sessions together.

General care

To stay happy, the Cocker Spaniel needs all the exercise an owner can possibly provide, particularly free running in woods and fields. It is especially important to take good care of its long ears. They need combing every day, and it's a good idea to feed your dog from a tall, narrow dish which keeps the ears out of the food. Carefully comb out any debris from the ears and coat after exercise and groom your Cocker at least once a week, checking the paws and inside the ears for hayseeds in the summer. They can cause infection if they are neglected.

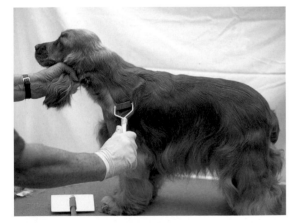

To groom a show dog, you can use a 'coat king' stripper, first on a coarse setting, then on a fine one for the dog's undercoat.

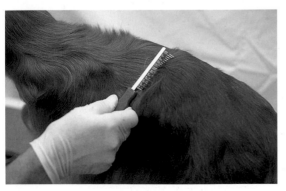

The Cocker Spaniel's coat needs regular combing to keep it silky and free from tangles.

English Springer Spaniel

One of the oldest recorded sporting dogs, the Springer Spaniel was first mentioned in literature by Chaucer. The word 'spaniel' may be derived from the Spanish word *Espangnol*. The Springer was developed in Britain during the nineteenth century and has become one of the world's great working gundogs.

must know

This breed suffers from some hip dysplasia, so ask to see the hip scores before buying a puppy. Eye problems include GPRA, CPRA and MRD. Make sure you buy a dog from tested parents.

Work

Springers are working gundogs with boundless energy. Their prime object is to 'spring' game from their hiding place for the shooters but they can also point and retrieve. They will enter the thickest cover fearlessly and leap into freezing water to retrieve a bird. Their extraordinary sense of smell has recently been exploited by police and customs who train Springers to sniff out drugs and explosives. They are also used as PAT dogs (visiting patients in hospital) and as Hearing Dogs for the Deaf.

Springers like nothing better than to be outside in the open air, in the park, garden or countryside.

Temperament

A gentle, loving dog whose natural desire is to please, the Springer is highly intelligent and reacts well to kind training. Being so energetic, however, these dogs can become a nuisance and develop undesirable behaviours, especially jumping up at people, without early training. Above all, they need things to occupy themselves and prevent boredom, especially retrieving games and play, and they take to Agility and Flyball with enthusiasm. Springers tend to be happy, friendly dogs and they crave and give affection, especially to their family. They hate being left alone and are good with children.

Springers love to play games and to chase and retrieve balls and other objects. They need plenty of exercise and running.

Appearance

The Springer is taller than the Cocker Spaniel with a weather-resistant coat and feathering on the ears, forelegs and hindquarters. The coat may be black and white, liver and white or one of these with tan markings. Dogs and bitches are approximately 50cm (20in) in height.

Opposite: Springers are energetic dogs and need all the exercise that you can possibly give them.

The Welsh Springer Spaniel comes only in a rich red and snow white, and it is slightly smaller than the English Springer.

Working and show lines

Note that as well as differences in temperament there are also physical differences between working Springers and show-type dogs. Thus the show line tends to be larger and heavier than its working counterpart with a differently shaped head, muzzle and ear set and length.

General care

Springers need plenty of free running and play on a daily basis to keep them happy and occupied as well as fit and healthy. They should be brushed and combed at least once a week. Trim the feathering with scissors and, most importantly, keep the ears dry and clean, especially after country walks.

must know

Strangers ✓✓✓
Will warn but friendly

Temperament ✓✓✓✓✓
Gentle and kind

Exercise ✓✓✓✓✓
A great deal daily

Grooming ✓✓✓
Weekly brushing, ears daily

Other dogs ✓✓✓✓
No problems

Summary
A loving family pet.

Pointer

Probably the greatest pointing breed, the Pointer's job is to quarter the ground, air scenting, and when it locates a bird to point to it by lining up its entire body, with the tail extended, neck stretched and one foreleg held up. It marks the bird for a long time, its body quivering with concentration.

must know

Strangers ✓✓✓
Very big bark, afterwards friendly

Temperament ✓✓✓✓✓
Gentle, affectionate, benign

Exercise ✓✓✓✓✓
Needs plenty but free running essential

Grooming ✓✓
Once or twice weekly; shed hair all the time

Other dogs ✓✓✓✓
Aloof but not unfriendly

Summary
Good gundog and pet

History

Some authorities believe that Pointers have existed in Britain since medieval times and were improved by the introduction of Spanish, Portuguese and French dogs in 1713 after the War of Spanish Succession. Other experts think it was the imported dogs, modified by the introduction of English Foxhound and Greyhound blood, that make up today's Pointer. This dog is a fast worker, and it is capable of scenting a sitting bird at distances of up to 200-250m. Although primarily a pointing breed, it can be taught to retrieve.

Temperament

The Pointer has a gentle, non-aggressive disposition not given to quarrelling with other dogs. It likes children but, because of its size, you must be careful about leaving one unattended with little ones. It is easy to train but has a stubborn streak and reacts badly to harsh treatment.

Appearance

A Pointer will point at an unseen bird with such concentration that it vibrates - every dog lover should witness the sight. It is a very handsome dog, muscular, symmetrical in form and gracefully curved, in lemon and white, orange and white, liver and white, or black and white (self colours and tricolours are fully acceptable). Dogs are 63–69cm (25–27in) in height; bitches are 61–66cm (24–26in).

General care

Condition is of the essence with this Olympic-style athlete and it is achieved with correct feeding by owners who are committed to giving their dog plenty of exercise. The Pointer's thin coat is 'easy care', requiring only a twice-weekly polishing with a hound glove. The breed does not thrive in cold, wet conditions, much preferring to be inside the house in the company of its owners.

must know

This breed is free of serious hereditary faults but there is some hip dysplasia in a few lines.

Pointers are muscular yet very graceful in appearance. They need a lot of exercise to keep them fit.

German Shorthaired Pointer

German hunters have a penchant for this powerful all-round gundog, which is capable of doing all three main tasks, making it a prime example of the genre – a Hunt, Point and Retrieve Gundog. It is often said in Germany: 'If a German Shorthaired Pointer cannot find it, it is not there'.

must know

Strangers ✓✓✓
Will warn loudly but not aggressive

Temperament ✓✓✓✓
Gentle and affectionate

Exercise ✓✓✓✓✓
This dog will take as much as you can give

Grooming ✓✓
Twice-weekly

Other dogs ✓✓✓✓✓
Friendly and sociable

Summary
Good all-round gundog and a gentle pet

History

This breed is an example of a designer dog. Up until the seventeenth century, the German Pointer was a heavy, slow dog known as a 'bird dog'. From 1870, great efforts were made by the Deutsche-Kurzhaar Verband, the German breed club, to produce the best possible gundog in both looks and efficiency. Using a variety of breeds, including the old Spanish, Wurttemberg and English Pointers with fast breeds from Scandinavia, they created and genetically fixed one of the great working gundogs.

Temperament

Generally happy and even-tempered, the German Shorthaired Pointer is not aggressive to other dogs. It has a kindly disposition towards children but should be kept away from small ones – big and bouncy, it might hurt them accidentally. Boisterous until three years old, this loyal, affectionate dog is devoted to its family but needs to be well trained.

Appearance

A medium-sized dog of sculptured appearance, when fit this dog's muscles should be well defined. The colour can be solid liver, liver with white spots and ticked, solid black or black and white spots, also ticked. The coat is short, flat and harsh to the touch. Dogs are 58-64cm (23-25in) in height while bitches are 53-59cm (21-23in).

General care

A breed as energetic as this one needs plenty of exercise, physical and mental. Without both, these dogs can become bored and even destructive. Best of all, a few days work in the shooting field will do them a power of good. They require training from a young age and, apart from natural field work, enjoy Agility or Flyball. Grooming is minimal – a rub over with a hound glove once or twice a week keeps the coat looking good (once daily when moulting). Do not feed a pet dog too much as they will incline to fat; more food is required if the dog is working. This is generally a healthy dog but there is a small amount of hip dysplasia in some lines.

must know

A trained Hunt, Point and Retrieve dog will hunt, follow a blood trail, quarter the ground and point and retrieve over any terrain as well as in water.

These handsome dogs have boundless energy and demand a lot of exercise and free running.

Weimaraner

Known as the 'grey ghost' because of its metallic, shimmering silver coat, this Hunt, Point and Retrieve (HPR) Gundog from Germany is different from other such dogs as it was developed to hunt big animals, including deer, bear, boar and wolf.

must know

Strangers ✓✓✓✓
Natural guard dog

Temperament ✓✓✓✓
Laid back, affectionate

Exercise ✓✓✓✓✓
Needs a vast amount, especially free running

Grooming ✓
Minimal: once a week

Other dogs ✓✓✓
OK if not threatened

Summary
Good pet and exceptional gundog; needs strong, fair handling. Tends to be a one-person dog

History

The origins of the Weimaraner are unknown; its ancestors may have been Bloodhounds, French Hounds and German Pointers. It came to the fore in 1810 with the Grand Duke Karl August of Weimar, Germany. The Weimaraner club was formed in 1897 with the breed kept exclusively for aristocrats. It was strictly monitored, and only puppies of the highest standard were permitted to live. Matings were carefully controlled.

It took an American, Howard Knight, nine years before he managed to acquire two bitches and a dog just before World War II. He, too, tried to control the breed but it became popular and was registered by the American Kennel Club in 1943. Weimaraners reached Britain in 1950.

Temperament

These friendly and obedient dogs need adequate socialization and firm but kind training while they are young because they can be very boisterous and self willed. They generally like children, although they are not particularly interested in them, so children must not disrespect them. They have an extraordinary sense of smell, excellent hearing and are good family guard dogs.

Appearance

A large muscular athlete with a short coat, the Weimaraner's unusual grey colouring gives the close-fitting coat a metallic sheen, which looks spectacular when it is moving in sunlight. Dogs are 61–69cm (24–27in) in height while bitches are slightly smaller – 56–64cm (22–25in).

General care

Without nourishing food, plenty of exercise and mental stimulation, this dog can become moody and destructive. It can be a town dog with plenty of walks or a country dog kept under strict control and not allowed to wander alone. It needs mental stimulation from training, play or the work for which it was developed. It's easy to groom, needing only a twice-weekly polish with a hound glove – daily during moulting. Pay attention to the ears.

must know

There is hip dysplasia in the breed, so check the breeder scores. There are other genetic disorders, none of which are considered to be very serious. Consult a responsible breeder.

This group of aloof-looking Weimaraners have the breed's distinctive silvery-grey coat.

Brittany

The intelligent Brittany is a versatile Hunt, Point and Retrieve (HPR) Gundog. Thus it will hunt like a hound, quarter the area, point like a Pointer and will retrieve on land or water.

must know

Strangers ✓✓✓
Will bark warnings but is not aggressive

Temperament ✓✓✓✓✓
Very sensitive, friendly and eager to please

Exercise ✓✓✓✓✓
Cannot give enough; needs play and free running

Grooming ✓✓✓
Three times a week; more when moulting

Other dogs ✓✓✓
Friendly

Summary
Versatile gundog and gentle family pet

History

Some authorities date this dog back to 150AD with a mention by the poet Oppien, but it is a tenuous link. Its known history starts in the nineteenth century, when it was fashionable for sporting aristocrats to go to Brittany in France to shoot partridge and snipe. They took their own Gundogs, including Pointers and English and Gordon Setters, which they often left behind to use the following season. The French mated them to their own extremely spirited Spaniel, the *Forgères*.

By 1900, the Brittany Spaniel, as it was known, was well established; it had a superb sense of smell, was inexhaustible, extremely brave in the face of harsh conditions and very biddable.

Temperament

This breed is extremely sensitive and it must have early socialization or it can be people shy. The Brittany is an energetic dog and it hates being left alone for long periods; thus some dogs will express their frustration by whining, barking and indulging in destructive behaviour. These dogs are fond of children, very affectionate and love to be part of all family activities. They excel at Obedience, Agility and Flyball, and are always eager to please, making them good family pets as well as gundogs.

Appearance

A square-built, muscular dog, the Brittany is taller than most other spaniels. It has a flattish, dense coat in orange and white, liver and white, black and white, tricolour or roan of any of these colours. Dogs are 48–50cm (19–20in) in height while bitches are 47–49cm (18–19in).

General care

Good walks with free running and games in the garden are essential for the pet Brittany. Deep grooming three times a week will keep the coat tangle free. Combing every day during the twice-annual moult will prevent the annoyance of having hair everywhere. This dog needs good nutritious food, and more than usual when it is working.

The Brittany needs careful handling as it can be sensitive and quite shy with strangers.

English Setter

Using dogs to assist in hunting for food is probably the oldest of all the canine professions. English Setters may well hold the record for being around a long time, and, although their origins are not recorded, bird-setting dogs such as these have been mentioned in literature since the 1500s.

must know

Strangers ✓✓✓
Will give warning

Temperament ✓✓✓
Friendly, good-natured

Exercise ✓✓✓✓
Plenty of walks and free running

Grooming ✓✓✓
Three times a week

Other dogs ✓✓✓✓✓
Happily socializes with all breeds

Summary
Affectionate family pet

Work

This dog works in concentric circles, head held high scenting the air. On detecting a bird, its nose goes down and it creeps very gently towards it as if it is hypnotised; the hunter moves in stealthily behind. Setters need careful and skilful training.

Temperament

A gentle and friendly dog, the English Setter is extremely affectionate and loves human company, although it will live happily in kennels provided it has companions. In general, the breed is very fond of children but they can be boisterous when young. Quiet in the house, a Setter will give warning of strangers but means them no harm.

Appearance

This dog has a soft expression and a noble carriage, which is noted for its symmetry – the basis of its elegance. It comes in several colours, all with white, black, orange, lemon, liver or tricolour. Those coats without heavy colour patches are preferred, but they should be flecked (known as Belton) all over. Dogs are 65-68cm (25-27in) in height, and bitches are 61-65cm (24-25$\frac{1}{2}$in).

General care

English Setters are immensely friendly dogs and they dislike being left alone. Feeding quality food in the correct amounts is essential, particularly for such an active breed; a higher calorific value is needed for working dogs. Plenty of exercise is very important for adults, especially when they are working because stamina is of the essence. It is a spirited and headstrong breed and must be trained with patience and kindness. The glamorous coat is maintained by tri-weekly attention, ensuring that the leg furnishings are combed to prevent tangles.

This English Setter has been prepared for showing and is being presented to the judge.

Irish Setter

The Irish have always been great sportsmen, and therefore it is not surprising that so many sporting dogs have emanated from Ireland, including this extremely active, glamorous-looking dog with its distinctive silky, rich red coat.

must know

There are some genetic anomalies which are closely monitored by the breed clubs, notably hip dysplasia, progressive retinal atrophy (PRA), CLAD and some bloat. Buy from those breeders who test their dogs via the KC/BVA tests and take their advice.

History

The Irish Setter's origins are not recorded. Small Spaniels that were used to find birds were bred with Bloodhounds to heighten their sense of smell. To increase their speed, the black Iberian and Spanish Pointers were introduced and thus the Irish Setter evolved. With the advent of dog shows, owners became obsessed with the glamour of the breed, but excessive inbreeding reduced the quality and it fell out of favour. By 1900 several British breeders reversed the tendency and dogs of great beauty appeared, a trend that holds good to this day.

Temperament

This boisterous but talented breed needs firm and kind control from an early age for Irish Setters are wilful and have a mind of their own. They should be socialized from puppyhood – this is best achieved at a dog training club. Gentle and tolerant of children, most Setters are kept as pets nowadays, although their passion for hunting is undiminished.

Appearance

The stunning rich red chestnut coat is the hallmark of the Irish Setter. It is a tall dog with elegant lines whose action, when running with a flowing coat, is a sight that once seen is never forgotten. Dogs are 60-70cm (23.5-27.5in) high, whereas bitches are 59-65cm (23-25.5in).

General care

A problem with this breed is how to provide enough exercise and stimulating activities to keep an adult dog busy. A country dog, it loves the open air and will run with joggers and cyclists. Do not let one off the lead in traffic or in the presence of livestock. Take care not to overfeed – this dog is an athlete. Groom it three times a week, taking care to gently comb the furnishings to prevent tangling.

These glamorous Irish Setters are parading around the show ring. Their spectacular coat and good looks make them popular pets.

Italian Spinone

The northern foothills and mountains of Italy have always been popular with Italian huntsmen because of the wild life intensity. Small wonder that they developed a superb Hunt, Point and Retriever (HPR) Gundog which could negotiate the harsh terrain, prickly undergrowth and marshland.

must know

Strangers ✓✓
Will give warning, but then friendly

Temperament ✓✓✓✓
Friendly but need firm handling

Exercise ✓✓✓✓✓
As much as you can possibly give, with free running

Grooming ✓✓
Twice a week

Other dogs ✓✓
Affable

Summary
Wonderfully amusing, very active but will calm down after adolescence

History

This is one of those rare dog breeds where some documentation from ancient times has survived – around 500BC and 100AD. It is possible that Roman soldiers brought a similar breed with them from Greece, or some could have been left behind by the Carthaginian Hannibal and merged with indigenous dogs. There are many theories but the only certain thing is it is an amalgam of several breeds.

Temperament

A happy, exuberant breed with an independent streak, Spinones need socialization and persistent,

Spinone puppies can be stubborn and they should be socialized and trained from an early age.

The shaggy Spinone is intelligent
and fun-loving. It makes a good
pet as well as a working dog.

careful training when young. They can be difficult
to house train and most are natural food thieves!
This is not a dog for the excessively house proud,
as they drool, moult, carry dirt into the house and
should not be left alone as they can be destructive.
However, they are really loving and adore children.

Appearance

The face is a cross between a cartoon dog and a
hairy guru. Very endearing as a puppy, the Spinone
grows into a big shaggy dog with a big personality.
Dogs are 60-70cm (23.5-27.5in) high while bitches
are 59-65cm (23-25.5in)

General care

Owners must have a commitment to exercise as
Spinones need all that is possible and then more, but
when out walking they can be deaf to all entreaties
when they scent something interesting. Greedy dogs,
they must not get overweight. Their coat has a natural
propensity to attract mud and debris and needs to be
groomed at least twice a week, more when moulting.

4 Terriers

All terriers originated in the British Isles. Many
hundreds of years ago they were nondescript
mongrels kept solely to control vermin around
farms and homesteads. As industrialization
occurred, these dogs were bred specifically
for working in mines, mills and factories.
Hunting practices changed and many regional
breeds evolved which are still in existence
today. Terriers now make good family pets
as they are affectionate, feisty and generally
healthy with great stamina and a real zest for
life. Some breeds, such as the Fox Terrier and
Kerry Blue Terrier, are now great show dogs,
winning many prizes.

Norfolk and Norwich Terriers

These two breeds share the same roots, which were probably in the fens of northern Norfolk and southern Cambridgeshire in the east of England. The fens were marshlands drained by canals and turned into rich agriculture land. Farmers liked to keep small terriers capable of killing the rats that ate into their profit.

must know

Strangers ✓✓✓
Will bark warning;
friendly dogs overall

Temperament ✓✓✓
Fun-loving, affectionate,
very active

Exercise ✓✓✓
At least two walks a day
plus garden play

Grooming ✓
Minimal: once a week

Other dogs ✓✓✓
No problems

Summary
Happy and vigorous
family dogs, full of
mischief and love

History

Nineteenth-century Cambridge undergraduates produced their own Trumpington Terriers for rat control and sport. Small Irish Terriers and large Yorkshire Terriers could also have been introduced. Jodrell Hopkins bred a litter of red puppies and he gave one named 'Rags' to the Master of the Norfolk Staghounds. Rags was a prick-eared red male, a great worker whose puppies were in demand. Frank Jones, First Whip to the Hunt, bought a few and began breeding and exporting them; in America his dogs were known as Jones Terriers. In the show rings both drop-ears and prick-ears were shown as one breed, the Norwich. They were not officially divided until 1964 when the prick-eared became the Norwich Terrier and the drop-eared the Norfolk Terrier.

Temperament

Sweet tempered and kindly disposed to everyone, these vibrant terriers are always full of energy and fun. Unhappy when left alone, they like to join in all family activities. Highly intelligent, easily trained but with a terrier's stubborn nature, they can conveniently forget what they have learnt. They are good with children but children must also be good with them.

Appearance

They are short-backed, short-legged chunky dogs – muscular and built for endurance. The coat is thick and harsh except for the head and ears. The Norfolk may be in shades of red, wheaten, black and tan and grizzle, whereas the Norwich is black, wheaten or any shade of brindle. In height, both dogs and bitches are 25–26cm (10in).

General care

These mischievous dogs need walking two or three times a day plus some strenuous play in the garden. Feeding presents no difficulties – the problem is how to stop these dogs getting fat, so no biscuits. Grooming consists of a good weekly brushing to get rid of dead hair and allow the new to grow through.

must know

These dogs have the occasional eye and liver problems, so check with The Kennel Club for the latest update.

Alert, curious and feisty, these vibrant little terriers love to play and make amusing companions.

Cairn Terrier

Many terriers were developed for working in specific regions of Great Britain, depending on the type of terrain and prey. Today's feisty, mischievous little Cairn Terrier is one of the few breeds that has not changed much in the last hundred years and still looks the same as depicted in old portraits.

must know

Strangers ✓✓
Will warn but generally friendly

Temperament ✓✓✓
Intelligent, playful and mischievous

Exercise ✓✓✓
At least two walks a day plus garden play

Grooming ✓✓
Twice a week

Other dogs ✓✓✓
Usually OK but some males like to dominate

Summary
Lovable, mischievous, and once bonded, always bonded

History

Small game terriers on the Scottish islands were known since 1500, and were a mixture of several different types. Only the best killers and guard dogs were retained, so, by selective breeding, little dogs kept the crofts comparatively free of rats, rabbits and foxes which lived in cairns (rock piles denoting boundaries and graves). Until the advent of dog shows, ordinary working people cared little about breeds, their size or colour; the criteria was if they did the job for which they were bred. The name 'Cairn' was not recognized by the Kennel Club, but Mrs Alistair Campbell, a breed enthusiast, persisted in exhibiting her 'Cairns' as 'Short-coated Skyes' and 'Prick-eared Skyes'. This so infuriated the Skye breeders that a delegation in 1910 persuaded the Kennel Club to accept the name 'Cairn'.

Temperament

The Cairn is a vibrant little dog, which is full of fun and mischief. It is very intelligent but training has to be patient and firm because it has an independent streak. Cairns are playful with children, but you must watch out for other small hairy pets like hamsters – these dogs still have their hunting instincts.

Appearance

Small but sturdy with rough, tousled hair, the Cairn Terrier always has prick ears. It is well muscled, giving the impression of agility, and can be cream, wheaten, red, grey or nearly black. Dogs and bitches are 28–31cm (11–12in) in height and should weigh 6–7.5kg (14–16lb).

General care

Cairns are tough but they need plenty of exercise to maintain their bodies and minds. They enjoy playing in a large garden, snuffling about under bushes and searching every mole hill. It is important, however, not to overfeed them as they can get fat. Grooming is minimal – just a brush and comb twice weekly.

Cairns may be small in stature but they more than make up for it in toughness and character.

West Highland White Terrier

This feisty, fun-loving little dog has become a very popular companion and family pet. Like all terriers, Westies are loving and loyal but fiercely independent. Their strength of character can make them strong-willed and stubborn at times, and they are not suitable pets for gentle, faint-hearted owners.

must know

Some eye problems are under investigation in Westies. They can also be susceptible to skin disorders, especially a type of eczema. Though it is quite rare, Legge Perthes disease can affect Westies, so check this out before you buy.

History

Up to the mid-1800s, the terriers of Scotland were a rough, hard, ill-disciplined and nondescript bunch controlling vermin on the small crofts. However, as foxhunting became fashionable, gentlemen began taking notice of terriers, although white dogs were not liked – some people thought they were not as game as coloured dogs. That changed when Colonel Edward Malcolm, thinking one of his own brown terriers was a fox as it emerged from an earth,

The West Highland White is a fun-loving little dog with a feisty and inquisitive character.

Opposite: Westies love to be involved in all family outings and activities. They hate being left behind at home.

must know

Strangers ✓✓✓
A good, alert guard

Temperament ✓✓✓✓
Playful, mischievous
and happy

Exercise ✓✓✓
Plenty of play and free
running

Grooming ✓✓✓✓
Frequent combing to
stop tangling; stripping
every three months

Other dogs ✓✓✓
Seldom picks a quarrel
but will defend itself

Summary
Family dog full of zest

accidentally shot it, and from then on he developed this unmistakable white terrier and was the breed club's first chairman in 1906. The Westie was used as an all-purpose worker and was kept as a 'vermin' killer or to hunt foxes, otters and wild cats. It had both stamina and courage and was agile enough to clamber over rocks and penetrate the smallest holes where its prey could hide.

Temperament

Feisty, stubborn, friendly, affectionate and playful, the Westie is a bright pet for town or country. Very few pet dogs can replicate this bundle of paradoxes: a fun dog that one minute will be digging up your

The Westie's head should be slightly domed with very dark, expressive eyes. The harsh, thick coat should be really white.

flower beds while hunting non-existent moles and the next minute will be lying on your lap with all the love of a spaniel. Because they were originally bred for hunting rats and foxes, they enjoy shaking and 'killing' their toys, especially squeaky ones.

Appearance

The Westie is a short-legged, square dog with a profuse wiry white coat, which needs some careful attention to maintain the typical shape. It has intensely dark intelligent eyes and small ears. The coat should be white without any brown marks. Dogs and bitches are 28cm (11in) in height.

General care

Twice-daily walks are essential for the active Westie, which also needs the freedom to run and play-hunt in a reasonably sized garden. To keep it in good condition, it will need stripping and shaping once every three months and combing on a daily basis.

Even pet Westies which are not shown need regular grooming to keep their coat in good condition.

It is important when grooming a Westie to brush the hair on the face downwards and then to brush it back up the other way.

Welsh Terrier

The Welsh Terrier is the only breed to win Best in Show at Crufts on four occasions. However, despite its glamorous appearance and image, like all terriers, it was bred originally to control rats.

must know

Strangers ✓✓✓
A good, alert guard

Temperament ✓✓✓✓
Affectionate, happy

Exercise ✓✓✓✓
Walks at least twice daily and free running

Grooming ✓✓✓
Combing twice weekly; hand-stripping every three or four months

Other dogs ✓✓✓
Non-aggressive but will defend itself

Summary
Loyal, friendly family pet

History

Today's Welsh Terrier emerged from the ubiquitous Broken-haired Black and Tan Terrier, which has been the basis of so many terrier breeds. Black and Tans have existed in Wales since medieval times and were written about by poets and bards. For years, they were virtually unknown outside Wales, because of the remoteness of the country, so breeding was close and type fixed.

The advent of railways and dog shows changed all that. Welsh Terriers found themselves competing against the mongrel Black and Tan Terriers, with some purporting to be Welsh Terriers. In 1885, the Welsh appealed to The Kennel Club for recognition of their breed, while the English appealed on behalf of theirs. The Kennel Club granted recognition to the Welsh Terrier but refused the English on the grounds that they did not breed true. The Welsh Terrier went on to become one of the biggest winning terrier breeds in the history of dog showing.

Appearance

A square, well-proportioned dog, deep-chested and muscular, the Welsh Terrier is built for running and jumping in the Welsh mountains and hunting for prey in the crevices and caves. It has a black and tan, weatherproof, wiry outer coat, which does not

Jaunty and highly intelligent, the Welsh Terrier is quite easy to train but can be very stubborn.

moult, and a woolly undercoat. Dogs and bitches should not exceed 39cm (15.5in) in height.

Temperament

This dog has a laid-back personality, not given to or seeking aggravation. It happily plays with any breed of dog but will give a good account of itself if it is attacked. Intelligent and good with children, it is not a noisy dog but is still a good guard. Quiet, patient training usually achieves good results. This is an affectionate dog who likes to be close to its family.

General care

This dog needs to be kept in hard condition, which is achieved by regular exercise. Walks two or three times a day, plus free running, games and training in the garden will keep it fit and stimulated, making for a more relaxed dog. The non-moulting coat can matt if neglected, but combing twice weekly prevents this. The coat should be hand stripped three or four times a year to preserve texture and colour; don't clip as this softens and lightens the colour.

must know

This robust terrier is comparatively free of genetic faults, although there are some rare cases of glaucoma.

Border Terrier

This breed evolved to work in the harsh weather conditions and over the difficult terrain of the Border Counties that lie between Scotland and England. Border Terriers have now become one of the most popular pet dogs throughout the world.

must know

Strangers ✓✓✓✓
Will warn, initially suspicious but then friendly

Temperament ✓✓✓✓
Laid back, affectionate

Exercise ✓✓✓✓✓
Needs plenty of physical exercise and mental stimulation

Grooming ✓
Minimal: once a week

Other dogs ✓✓✓
If not well socialized, some dogs can become over-dominant

Summary
A quiet, affectionate pet but a great escapologist, so gardens must be 100 per cent secure

History

Small terriers capable of working with hounds have been bred in the Border Counties for over 200 years. The Lowther family bred Border Terriers in 1723, and Lord Lonsdale had a painting of the Cottesmore hounds with a brace of Border Terriers painted in 1693. What constituted the breed is still in question: the now extinct Old Lyne and Reedwater Terriers with a touch of early Bedlington and Dandie Dinmont are contenders. It was a question of preference, and there were several breeds, all hard and workmanlike, which were working on the border. Two masters of different hunts, Dodd and Robson, whose families inter-married, were largely responsible for the development of the Border Terrier. The breed was eventually recognized by The Kennel Club in 1920 but its enthusiasts have maintained its hunting qualities.

Temperament

This dog combines docility with intelligence with humans but it is fiercely uncompromising when working. The Breed Standard confirms its working qualities above and below the ground. As pets, these terriers are affectionate but undemonstrative and good with children. They are fairly easy to train but are offended if shouted at.

Borders enjoy hunting and they are never happier than when they pick up a scent and follow it.

Appearance

This small terrier gives the impression of compressed power and agility. The small folded ears and short muzzle are not unlike an otter's head. They have a weatherproof, thick, harsh coat with a close undercoat, and a thick protective skin. They can come in red, wheaten, grizzle and tan or blue and tan. Dogs should weigh 5.9–7kg (13–15.5lb); bitches 5.1–6.1kg (11.5–14 lb). For height, calculate 2.5cm (1in) per 450g (1lb) in weight. They should not be allowed to get fat; both sexes should be capable of being spanned by both hands behind the shoulder.

This game little dog needs lots of exercise. It enjoys free running, lead walking and hunting for rats.

General care

Fairly easy to rear, Border Terriers are not given to greediness but to keep them slim, do avoid sweet treats. Increase the protein in their diet if they are working. Exercise is vastly important: they need two or three walks a day with free running. Games in a large garden are ideal to stimulate the brain. Hand stripping three times a year with grooming once or twice a week will keep the coat looking good.

must know

The Border is free of serious genetic anomalies but slight possibility of eye disorders is currently under investigation.

Fox Terrier (Wire and Smooth)

To all intents and purposes, the two breeds are identical except for the coat type and ideal weight. They are also very similar in temperament, so which you choose depends on your personal preference and the time you can spend on grooming your dog.

must know

Strangers ✓✓✓
A good, alert guard

Temperament ✓✓✓✓
Playful, mischievous and fairly easy to train

Exercise ✓✓✓
Plenty of play and free running

Grooming ✓✓✓✓
Daily for Wire coat; once a week for Smooth coat

Other dogs ✓✓✓
Happy with all breeds but will not tolerate threats

Summary
Fun dogs, a joy to own

History

At the end of the eighteenth century, foxhunting became the pastime of the gentry, and a small, white, courageous dog able to go to earth and run with the hounds was a requirement. By selective breeding by huntsmen using available terriers and introducing the Beagle, Foxhound, Bull Terrier and other breeds, recognizable Smooth Fox Terriers began to emerge. Wire-haired puppies appeared in the same litters but were not popular. Fashions changed with the advent of dog shows, and as owners of Wire-haired dogs realized they could be trimmed attractively and win in competition, the Wire-haired overtook the Smooth in popularity.

Appearance

The Smooth Fox Terrier is small, well balanced, muscular but symmetrical. It has a lean head with folded ears, straight legs and a level topline with a straight tail carried vertically. It has short, harsh hair, white predominating with tan, black and tan or black markings. The Wire has the same bodily characteristics but the coat is wiry and presented shortish on the body, with a beard and eyebrows; the legs should be furnished with hair. Dogs should not exceed 39cm (15^1/$_2$in), bitches slightly less.

Temperament

After socializing and basic training, both breeds are playful and mischievous, wanting to join in family activities. Intelligent and fairly easy to train, they have an independent streak. Although they are very good with children, they may play roughly. They will guard and warn of a stranger's approach.

General care

Plenty of exercise is essential as they are natural athletes and need things to do or they will find something that is undesirable to you. Chasing a ball in the garden is good, especially if they have to look for it. Grooming the Smooth is easy – brushing once a week followed by a rub with a hound glove. The Wire coat should be combed daily to prevent tangles and stripped three or four times a year.

The Smooth Fox Terrier requires considerably less grooming than its Wire-haired counterpart.

Mischievous and jaunty, the Wire has a feisty nature and, like all terriers, is fiercely independent.

Kerry Blue Terrier

The Irish dog breeders have long been famed for the quality of their indigenous breeds, and the spectacular Kerry Blue Terrier has become a great show dog as well as a fun-loving family pet.

must know

Strangers ✓✓✓✓✓
Serious guard dog, suspicious of strangers

Temperament ✓✓✓✓
Laid back, affectionate

Exercise ✓✓✓✓✓
Must have plenty: running, walking and play

Grooming ✓
Combing daily but clipping every three to four months

Other dogs ✓✓
Be careful: this breed is quick to take offence

Summary
Revels in human companionship; difficult with strange dogs unless well socialized

History

There is a myth that a dog which was washed up from a shipwreck subsequently mated with a local bitch and produced a blue dog, but the origins of the Kerry Blue Terrier are unknown; most experts think it stems from the Soft-coated Wheaten Terrier. The Kerry Blue used to be a farm dog, eking out a precarious existence in Kerry in the Republic of Ireland, until it came to the public's notice after World War I because one was owned by Michael Collins, the leader of the Irish rebels. Young men supporting him kept the breed as an icon of their defiance against the British. The English Kennel Club refused to recognize the breed, so the Kerry Blue fanciers created their own club and formed the Irish Kennel Club when it became popular at shows.

Appearance

Rectangular in profile, the Kerry Blue is a medium to large sized muscular dog, which is instantly recognizable due to the unique blue/grey colour of its coat. These terriers are born black and their coat gradually changes to blue by the time they are approximately six months old. Dogs are 46–48cm (18–19in) in height and bitches are slightly smaller. The ideal weight for dogs is 15–16.8kg (33–37lb); 15.9kg (35 lb) for bitches.

Temperament

This warm-hearted, boisterous Irishman makes an affectionate companion and will keep all varieties of vermin at bay. It can be sharp with other dogs but to its humans it is a delight. Be careful with little children as this dog can play quite roughly. It needs good socialization and early training.

General care

This is not a breed for the novice owner. Exercise is of prime importance to take the edge off the Kerry Blue's boisterous nature, and kindly training is essential to keep it under control. An owner must also be committed to keeping the coat in order; it needs daily combing to prevent tangles and keep the beard clean, as well as professional scissoring once every three months to maintain the short curly look which is the escutcheon of the breed.

must know

Apart from rare hip dysplasia in some lines, this breed is remarkably free of serious genetic disorders.

This Kerry Blue has been prepared for showing. Although they are big winners in the showing world, these dogs have not lost their terrier instincts.

Parson Jack Russell Terrier

This lively breed was developed for active work and would suit an energetic owner who enjoys exercising. If you want a canine companion for when you go out jogging or you fancy joining an Agility or Flyball class, then this is the right dog for you.

This is a fun dog for all the family. Faithful and affectionate, it loves to be busy and has boundless energy. Give it as much exercise, play and time as possible.

Opposite: The Parson Jack Russell is always on the look out for prey, including vermin, squirrels, birds, rabbits, moles and even hares.

History

Parson Jack Russell was a cleric, who was rather unjustly more famed for his hunting exploits than for his pastoral work. Born in Devon in 1795, he took a good degree at Oxford and was ordained in 1819. As a student, he annoyed the college authorities by keeping an illicit small pack of hounds, and it was whilst he was up at Oxford that he acquired the bitch terrier that was to become the foundation of the breed that was named after him.

Strolling in Magdalen Meadow one day, Jack Russell met the local milkman and saw, for the first time, the terrier named Trump. He did not move until he had persuaded the milkman to part with her. He died at 84 years old, still in the saddle, and with his breed of dogs a fitting memorial.

Temperament

Highly intelligent, the busy Parson Jack Russell is always doing things and is very affectionate as well as being a good guard dog – alert and watchful. Their wonderful friendly nature blossoms within a happy family and they are extremely patient with children. This is an easily-trained, fun dog which is into everything. However, it does need to be busy and active and can easily become bored.

The smooth-coated Parson Jack
needs minimal grooming – just a
quick brush with a rubber slicker.

Small-legged Jack Russells are
now becoming more popular
as family pets, but they are not
recognized by the Kennel Club.

Work

This is a working terrier, which is reflected in the
Breed Standard. The Jack Russell must have the
conformation to go to earth and run with hounds.
Its job is to either mark the fox underground or
bolt it, so it needs courage without recklessness
coupled with stamina. It is also one of the great
ratters with razor-sharp reactions.

Appearance

The Parson Jack Russell is a small athletic
dog which is full of vitality. It is slightly longer
than its height at the shoulders – 35cm (14in)
for dogs; 33cm (13in) for bitches. The wiry
or smooth coat is mostly white with black
and/or tan patches. Note that the long-legged
Parson Jack Russell Terrier should not be
confused with the smaller-legged Jack Russell
Terrier, which is now much more common but
is not recognized by The Kennel Club.

General care

There are two types of coat: the smooth variety requires only a weekly brush whereas the rough coat needs hand stripping or trimming every four to five months as well as weekly brushing. This is a country dog needing plenty of exercise, free running and mental stimulation. Unless you have the space and are prepared to spend a lot of time exercising it, this is not a suitable dog for you.

Teaching your dog games and tricks will help to exercise it physically and mentally, making it less likely to develop any behaviour problems. It enjoys playing games but will get very excited and will shake and 'kill' toys that squeak. Beware if you are a keen gardener with carefully planted flowerbeds as this dog loves digging!

Strangers ✓✓✓
A very watchful dog;
intruders beware

Temperament ✓✓✓✓✓
Happy-go-lucky fun dog,
intelligent and trainable

Exercise ✓✓✓✓
Running and playing
as much as possible

Grooming ✓✓✓
Smooth-haired needs
minimal grooming;
rough-haired needs
brushing

Other dogs ✓✓
Not aggressive but will
stand their ground

Summary
Ideal for the dynamic
country family

The long-legged Parson Jack likes nothing better than to be outside hunting or free running.

Airedale Terrier

The largest of all the terrier breeds, this is yet another designer dog bred by working men for specific purposes. Airedales make grand companions and show dogs, winning at the highest level.

History

During the Industrial Revolution, many agriculture workers lost their land and went to the Yorkshire mills and mines to earn a living. New industries were situated on the rivers Aire and Wharfe and the workers wanted a large, courageous all-purpose dog for hunting and fighting. By selective breeding, they created the Airedale. We do not know which breeds constitute Airedales; they probably started with the Black and Tan broken-haired Terrier and added the Bull Terrier and Otterhound. Originally named Waterside Terriers, they appeared in the 1886 Kennel Club Stud Book as Airedales. They became hunting dogs, police dogs and war dogs as well as pets.

Appearance

This big dog is usually prepared in a similar way to a Welsh Terrier with a beard and eyebrows, the coat cut close on the body with furnishings on the legs. The coat should be extremely wiry with a soft undercoat. The colour is always black and tan. Dogs are 58–61cm (23–24in) in height, while bitches are less tall at 56–59cm (22–23in).

The powerful Airedale is the largest of all the terriers. Exuberant and fun-loving, it can be quite noisy and will bark to warn of visitors and intruders.

Temperament

This reliable, kindly dog has a great affection for its family, is very playful and loves children. However, because of its size, be careful with small children. Although relatively easy to train, it has a streak of independence in its character. Its calm nature means that it is not given to being aggressive to other dogs, but it will be a very effective guard.

General care

Like other canine athletes, Airedales need plenty of exercise, and playing in a large garden will help keep them alert. They are also adapt at Agility and Flyball. Although they do not moult, they need brushing and combing weekly; if neglected, the hair tangles and matts. For competition, the wiry coat must be hand stripped. Pet dogs are usually professionally trimmed once every three to four months.

must know

Strangers ✓✓✓✓
A good, alert guard

Temperament ✓✓✓✓
Playful, reliable but can be stubborn

Exercise ✓✓✓✓
Plenty of walks, free running and play

Grooming ✓✓✓✓
At least once a week; hand stripping or trimming every three to four months

Other dogs ✓✓✓
Non-aggressive but will defend itself

Summary
A lovely, warm family member who wants nothing more than to be involved in everything

Airedales have an intelligent, alert expression and distinctive 'beard' which needs regular cleaning and grooming.

Staffordshire Bull Terrier

As a breed, the 'Staffie' is a comparative newcomer, but its antecedents probably go back 6,000 years as it belongs to an exclusive club of Mastiff-style dogs, which were bred game enough to fight against all odds on the bidding of their masters.

Strangers ✓✓✓✓✓
A forceful deterrent

Temperament ✓✓✓✓
Easy-going, happy clown

Exercise ✓✓✓✓
Walking, running and play essential

Grooming ✓
Very little; use a hound glove to polish

Other dogs ✓✓✓✓✓
Not confrontational but will never back down

Summary
A wonderful family dog; not for the novice owner

History

The ancestors of the modern Staffie once fought in battles shoulder to shoulder with soldiers; they fought wild animals in Roman times; and later bulls, bears, rats and, finally, each other. The Duke of Hamilton, a sporting rake of around 1770, set out to develop a lighter fighting dog – the big Bulldogs not being fast enough – which is claimed to be the forerunner of the breed today. At the end of the eighteenth century, it was simply the best fighting dog around. However, it was not until the 1930s that a Breed Standard was created and the Staffie became a show dog and companion.

Even though it is very muscular and powerfully built, the Staffie is an energetic and agile dog.

Temperament

Fearless, people-friendly and intelligent, Staffies must be disciplined and trained. This is relatively easy but patience is needed. Despite its bloody history, it is, today, one of the most faithful, affectionate, family-loving pets. A Staffie will fiercely guard babies and is good with older children when they show respect.

Appearance

This chunky, well-muscled, medium-small dog has a wide head, a pump handle tail and walks with a jaunty air. The smooth coat is red, fawn, white, black or blue. Height is related to weight and most dogs are 35.5–40.5cm (14–16in) tall.

General care

Grooming is minimal; all that is needed is a brush and polish weekly to get rid of dead hairs. Staffies need both physical and mental stimulation, with plenty of exercise, including free running and play.

The Staffie has a wide, deep chest and straight forelegs.

must know

Generally a healthy breed but buy from eye-tested parents and have your puppy tested.

Affectionate and extremely loyal, Staffordshire Bull Terriers make good family pets if they are well socialized and trained as puppies.

Bull Terrier

The Bull Terrier is a classic example of a skilful dog breeder taking a rough and ready fighting dog and changing it into an elegant breed, which was suitable as a pet for Victorian gentlemen.

must know

Strangers ✓✓✓✓✓
Excellent guard dog

Temperament ✓✓✓✓
Laid back, affectionate

Exercise ✓✓✓✓✓
Needs a lot of daily exercise and play

Grooming ✓
Minimal: once a week

Other dogs ✓✓✓
This dog does not seek arguments but will not back down

Summary
Strong willed but sweet nature; not a dog for the faint hearted

History

Although in 1835, bull fighting, bear baiting, dog fighting and other cruel sports were made illegal in Britain, dog fighting continued in secret. The dogs used were Bulldogs crossed with terriers, known as Bull-and-Terriers. James Hinks, a dog dealer and breeder, introduced the English White Terrier (now extinct) and Dalmatian to create a more attractive dog. Hinks showed his new type, an all-white bitch named Puss, in London in 1862, competing against the Bull-and-Terriers. When mocked and challenged to fight one of the old type dogs, Puss fought and killed the other dog in half an hour. Unmarked, she returned to the show and won her class as well as 'Best Conditioned Dog'. The breed became a popular pet and show dog. Coloured Bull Terriers were introduced and after 1950 were accepted as equals.

Appearance

The hallmark of this breed is the unique egg-shaped head with its small triangular eyes and prick ears. The body is athletically muscled, showing great power. The coat is short, harsh to the touch and close fitting. Colours are pure white, brindle, black, red fawn and tricolour. No height or weight is given but the dog should give the impression of maximum substance consistent with its quality and sex.

must know

Hereditary deafness and heart problems have been reported in this breed.

Although they were originally bred for fighting, Bull Terriers are good-natured dogs and they enjoy human company.

Temperament

If disciplined and trained with kindness from puppies, these dogs become responsive to human affection, are full of fun and make faithful family pets which are good with children. They are also natural guard dogs; they will not start a fight but will finish one!

General care

Unless an owner is prepared to devote some time daily to training and exercising this dog, it is not the breed for them. It is the ultimate canine athlete and needs plenty of exercise, or it can be destructive. Feeding presents no difficulties but it must not be overfed. Grooming is easy: just a good brushing twice a week, and cleaning the ears and feet. They like to be warm and dry; always towel-dry them thoroughly after they have been out in the rain.

want to know more?

• For more information on terriers, see The Kennel Club's book on Breed Standards
• Contact the terrier breed clubs and societies via the Internet
• If you are interested in doing Flyball and Agility with your terrier, go to www.thekennelclub.org.uk

5 Utility dogs

This group of dogs includes some of our most popular companion breeds, including the Dalmatian, Lhasa Apso, Poodle and Shih Tzu. Some of these utility dogs were once used for guarding and warning of any approaching strangers, or even for fighting, as in the case of the Bulldog. However, now they make excellent family pets, offering us both their companionship and entertainment.

Boston Terrier

Although this dog may be relatively small in stature, it more than makes up for this in its character. Lively and determined, the strong-willed Boston Terrier is easily recognizable with its distinctive pricked ears and large expressive eyes.

must know

Only buy a puppy from eye-tested parents. There is some slipping patella in this breed.

History

Around 1865 in Cotter's tavern in Charles Street, Boston, USA, coach drivers, stable men and ostlers used to gather together whilst their masters were attending functions. They wondered what the result would be if they mated together some of the fine imported pedigree dogs belonging to the gentry together. Thus Bulldogs were mated to Bull Terriers and then to Pit Bull Terriers, and the result was a fighting dog weighing up to 27kg (60lb). The Boston Terrier's strange beauty was recognized and then selectively bred to create a smaller dog. In 1891, the breeders formed a club and created a Standard, and the Boston Terrier is now one of America's favourite dogs.

Temperament

An amiable, docile dog, the highly intelligent Boston Terrier is easily trained, full of character and a good guard dog. Although it is now just a

Boston Terriers make good companions as they are easy-going and fun-loving dogs.

The Boston Terrier's large ears are held erect and the eyes have an alert but gentle expression.

well-behaved house pet, it was bred originally as a fighting dog. A boisterous dog, the Boston Terrier is full of fun with a penchant for playing with toys.

Appearance

A muscular, small, square dog, the Boston Terrier has a big head and a short muzzle. His large 'bat ears' are his trademark. The coat colour should be brindle with white markings for preference, but black with white is acceptable. Dogs come in three sizes: from below 6.8kg (15lb) to 11.4kg (25lb).

General care

Hardly any grooming is required for this dog – just a soft brush and polish once a week. Two or three good walks a day together with some free running and playtime in the garden are all the exercise a Boston Terrier needs. The prominent eyes are easily damaged, so keep the dog out of bushes.

must know

Strangers ✓✓✓✓
Very good guard; the 'bat ears' miss nothing

Temperament ✓✓✓✓
A tractable dog, happy and friendly

Exercise ✓✓✓
A couple of walks a day and a bit of play

Grooming ✓
Just a weekly brush and take care of the eyes

Other dogs ✓✓✓
A non-aggressive dog; never seeks trouble

Summary
An easy-going character bringing pleasure

Bulldog

The Bulldog, which has become emblematic of British courage and endurance, is one of the most ancient of all the British breeds. Although it looks fierce, it is genial and intensely loyal and makes an affectionate family pet.

History

We don't know when this breed appeared in Britain; in ancient times it went under different names – Alaunt, Mastive and Bandogge. These dogs had big heads, short muzzles, incredible courage and an ability to 'pin and hold'. In 1204, Lord Stamford of Lincolnshire saw butchers' dogs tormenting a bull, found it entertaining and offered a field for bull baiting. Bulls' horns were padded and dogs were tossed in the air, the spectators standing close to catch them before they hit the ground. Dog fighting became illegal in 1835 and the breed, now known as the Bulldog, began to lose its popularity but was still exhibited. In 1874, the Bulldog Club was formed and people became interested in improving the breed. As dog shows became popular, so did the Bulldog.

Temperament

The late Bulldog breeder Mrs E.E. Smith's words on the temperament of the Bulldog cannot be bettered: 'The Bulldog's apparent stolidity, stemming from his forbidding exterior covers many sterling qualities…abundant affection, kindness, especially to children, reluctance to fight but courageous and steadfast if he has to. Unparalleled loyalty coupled with an unfailing sense of humour.'

Grooming a bulldog is simple: just weekly brushing and keeping the wrinkles and ears clean. Always dry them after exercising in rain.

Appearance

This dog has a wide head with a short muzzle and wrinkle, giving a fierce aspect, heavily-muscled, short legs and a wide chest. The coat of short hair comes in different colours: whole or smut (whole colour with black mask or muzzle) in brindles, various shades of red, white and pied. Dogs should weigh 26kg (55lb) and bitches 22.7kg (50lb).

General care

Bulldogs need to be exercised regularly for short distances when young, increasing as they grow, in the coolest part of the day. Keeping them slim is very important: the type of food and quantity should be controlled. Grooming is simple – just brushing weekly and keeping the wrinkles and ears clean.

must know

There are genetic problems, so buy only from breeders who are members of the integrated health scheme that monitors respiratory disability, eye and joint anomalies. To find out more, go to www.bulldogbreed council.co.uk

Lhasa Apso

Although in the West, Lhasa Apsos are bred as companions or show dogs, in their native land they are watchdogs, often sitting in a high place where they can keep an eye on the comings and goings of the monks and warning of the approach of strangers.

must know

This breed is generally tough as befits a dog that has evolved in the harsh, cold climate of the Tibetan mountains. Some eye conditions are under investigation, so buy from tested parents.

History

High in the mountains of Tibet, monks bred this little dog as a watchdog and companion before the birth of Christ. It may have evolved from Central European herding dogs, such as the Pumi or Puli. The breed was regarded as a talisman and, although they were never sold, they were often gifted to the Chinese nobility. In 1904, a few dogs were brought from Tibet to the West, and in the early 1920s a Mrs Bailey and other ladies bred from these dogs to form the nucleus of the breed in Britain.

These puppies will eventually have a heavy adult coat.

Temperament

Although wary of strangers, the Lhasa Apso is loving with its human family without being too effusive. As a sole dog, it will probably bond with one person in the family very strongly but it also has a very independent streak and tends to be quite aloof, so it may not be so clingy as some people like their pet dogs to be.

Appearance

This short-legged, long dog has a profuse and heavy coat which comes in several colours, including shades of gold,

In Tibet, the Lhasa Apso's name means 'hairy barking dog'. It is a good guard dog, barking at strangers.

dark grizzle, smoke, parti-colour, black, white or brown. Dogs are 25cm (10in) in height, whereas bitches tend to be slightly smaller.

General care

This tough little dog is full of energy and is able to walk long distances. However, it can be happy with several short walks. The crowning glory of the breed is its glorious coat, which does need daily attention, otherwise it will tangle and matt. The coat can be kept short if you don't intend showing the dog.

This champion show dog with its marvellous heavy coat is in superb condition. It needs grooming every day to keep it looking good.

Poodle

Most people associate Poodles with the glamour of the show ring, but they were originally bred as working retrievers and are the most active of breeds. They love work of all kinds, excelling at Agility, Obedience and Flyball.

This fashionable dog was originally bred as a working water breed.

must know

Standard Poodles have a low incidence of hip dysplasia. Puppies from all varieties should come from eye-tested parents.

History

Like so many ancient breeds, the Poodle has its origins in hunting. The breed comes from Germany, the name 'Pudel' derived from *puddeln*, meaning to 'splash in water'. The French name *Caniche* is derived from *chien-canne*, meaning a 'duck dog', as the Poodle was a wildfowler. The development of the three varieties as pet dogs began in the 1800s. The Belgians liked big white dogs for hauling milk carts, whereas the French bred small whites, and the Russians liked black miniatures. Although it is doubtful if any Poodles are used as retrievers any more, they betray their wildfowling antecedents by their joy in retrieving games.

Temperament

A loving, sensitive breed possessed of superior intelligence, the Poodle becomes totally involved with family activities, particularly with children. It is a sheer delight for novices to experienced dog lovers; if the Poodle is trained with kindness it will be an obedient and much-loved family pet.

Appearance

Poodles have a springy movement and invariably look proud and happy. The Miniatures and Toys look

like small versions of the Standard. They come in all solid colours and the hairdressing styles vary according to taste, the lion and lamb clips being most often seen. Standard Poodles are 38cm (15in) in height; Miniatures are under 38cm (15in); and Toys are 28cm (11in).

General care

All Poodle varieties have an unbounded energy and will take more exercise and play than you can give. Poodles do not moult but they must be combed every other day to prevent tangles. Unless you are a hairdresser it is better to take the dog to the grooming parlour four or five times a year than clip it yourself.

The way in which a Poodle is clipped reflects is role as a water dog and is designed to protect the joints in cold water and help buoyancy.

Schnauzer

The modern Schnauzer is usually a much-loved family pet and does not generally have work to do, but it still retains the will and ability of its ancestor, an all-round farm dog. Some European countries use these dogs as guard dogs – a role they relish.

must know

Generally, the modern Schnauzer is a healthy, hard breed with few health problems.

History

The Schnauzer was almost certainly derived from the ancient Wire-haired Pinscher to which it bears a startling resemblance as seen in a picture by Albrecht Dürer (1492). A fourteenth-century statue of a hunter in Mechlinburg, Germany, has a similar dog crouched at his feet. This old breed was a general farm dog, keeping down rats, hunting and protecting its owners. It was known to accompany stagecoaches in order to defend them against the robbers who worked the forests and thus it became known as the 'Carriage Griffon'.

The dense wiry coat will need to be brushed and combed thoroughly twice every week.

Although this dog may look fierce and is very protective of its family, it has a very friendly nature.

Temperament

Absolutely devoted to its family, the Schnauzer is a happy dog which can be trained relatively easily to be obedient. There is no need to worry about your property or children if this fellow lives with you; it is an outstanding watchdog. Courageous and assertive, it is a good companion but needs strong but kind handling.

Appearance

A chunky, medium-sized muscular dog, the coat is black or pepper and salt (greyish) in colour. The outer coat is wiry, harsh to the touch and distinguished by a beard and bushy eyebrows; the undercoat is dense. Dogs are 48cm (19in) high; bitches are 46cm (18in).

General care

Schnauzers require frequent running exercise and play in order to maintain their athleticism and mental health. The wire coat needs hand stripping four times a year, and the leg and face furnishings should be combed out twice a week.

must know

Strangers ✓✓✓✓✓
Suspicious, prowlers beware

Temperament ✓✓✓✓
Affectionate family dog, brave, caring deeply

Exercise ✓✓✓✓✓
Enough to keep muscle tone

Grooming ✓✓✓✓✓
Hand stripped quarterly

Other dogs ✓✓✓
Males can be dominant

Summary
All-round family pet

Miniature Schnauzer

The Miniature variety is the most popular of the three Schnauzer breeds, particularly in America where its final development took place. Because of their working antecedents, Mini Schnauzers are very active and keen on doing things, particularly activities with their owners such as Agility, Obedience and Flyball.

must know

This is a hardy little dog but puppies should be bought from eye-tested parents and should be tested themselves in the fullness of time.

Intelligent and very sensitive, this game little dog makes a good companion for all the family.

History

A manufactured breed with its foundation in the Standard Schnauzer, this was exhibited as a breed by itself in 1879 in Germany. It has been suggested that as well as the Wire-haired Pinscher, the blood of the Affenpinscher also runs through its veins. The combination of these two breeds may well be the reason that Mini Schnauzers are the only one of the three breeds to be described as ratters.

Temperament

Affable, sensitive and extremely intelligent, the Mini Schnauzer learns its manners very quickly, suiting all homes, especially those with young children. An excellent pet dog which learns quickly what is expected of it, it is small enough to be carried but is not a toy. These dogs are very playful and get on well with other animals and children.

Appearance

This small square dog has a wire coat and profuse furnishings on the legs, a distinctive beard and lowering eyebrows. The coat colour is pepper and salt (greyish), black or a striking black and silver. The dogs are 35cm (14in) in height whereas the bitches are 33cm (13in).

General care

This breed tends to overweight, so Mini Schnauzers must be exercised. They will take as much as an owner is prepared to give although smaller amounts are acceptable. The dog's coat requires particular attention and it should be hand stripped about four times a year. The furnishings and beard must be combed out at least two or three times every week.

must know

Strangers ✓✓✓✓
Slightly suspicious;
a good guard dog

Temperament ✓✓✓✓✓
Loving, easy-going
happy, playful pet

Exercise ✓✓✓
Will run ten miles or
take less

Grooming ✓✓✓✓✓
Hand stripping four
times yearly; furnishings
combed frequently

Other dogs ✓
Not quarrelsome

Summary
Ideal dog for a young
and active family

A Miniature Schnauzer's distinctive long beard and furnishings on the legs need frequent brushing and combing to keep the coat in good condition.

Shih Tzu

Shih Tzus are first and foremost a companion dog; they like to be out and about with their owners and fully integrated within all family activities. However, they are alert watchdogs and will not let any strange noise pass without marking it.

must know

The Shih Tzu is generally a very healthy dog. Some pinched noses can cause breathing problems, so check the puppy's parents.

Both enthusiastic and remarkably intelligent, the Shih Tzu makes a very loyal and friendly family pet.

History

This breed's Chinese name, Shih Tzu Kou, means 'Lion dog'. Its origins are in Tibet where it enjoyed the status of a 'holy dog' as far back as the seventh century. These dogs were sometimes presented to visiting foreign dignitaries, which is probably how they entered China. After the death of the empress Tzu-hsi in 1908, the breed deteriorated and the best stock was sold. Outside China there was confusion as Shih Tzus were mixed with Apsos and were given different names. The first three dogs came to Great Britain in 1930, and by 1934 Lhasa Apsos and Shih Tzus were recognized as different breeds.

Temperament

An amusing, independent pet which fades away without human companionship, this is undoubtedly a fun dog, bouncy with a great enthusiasm for life. A very intelligent, happy companion, the loyal Shih Tzu presents no problems in the home but, craving human contact, it dislikes being left alone, so don't consider owning one if you are out at work for most of the day. It tends to be quite aloof with strangers and people it does not know well.

Appearance

A short-legged dog with a muscled body under a profuse flowing coat, sometimes trailing down to the floor, the Shih Tzu comes in any colour, but a white blaze on the forehead and tail tip is much admired in parti-colours. While the top coat is very silky, the undercoat is quite dense. Some owners keep their dogs in a 'puppy clip' with the hair cut to about 5cm (2in). Dogs and bitches should not exceed 27cm (11in) high.

General care

Two walks a day and playing in the garden will suffice for this game little dog. The main attraction of the breed is the magnificent coat, but do not consider taking on a Shih Tzu unless you are prepared for all the work that is needed to maintain it. The hair knots and tangles quite easily and it requires daily attention. It should be kept clean and conditioned.

Dalmatian

Nowadays Dalmatians are solely companion dogs and they are rarely used for work, but this was not always the case. They were once commonly known as 'carriage dogs' and they would run for miles under a carriage between the wheels or beside the horses.

must know

Strangers ✓✓✓
Will warn off intruders

Temperament ✓✓✓✓✓
Devoted, anxious to
please its owners

Exercise ✓✓✓✓✓
Cannot get enough

Grooming ✓
A weekly brush up

Other dogs ✓✓✓✓
Generally friendly

Summary
Ideal for an active
country family

History

We don not know the origin of this dog's name; almost certainly it is not from Dalmatia on the coast of what was once Yugoslavia. Spotted dogs have been present in Europe for centuries as proved by numerous paintings. This breed was a farm dog and it has a strange affinity with horses. From the eighteenth century until the mid-nineteenth century, they lived roughly in the gentry's stables keeping down rats and guarding the premises. Their graceful shape and striking colour attracted the attention of fashionable young bucks of the day who delighted in using them to ornament their carriages.

Temperament

These dogs love the company of humans and are affectionate and anxious to please. Being essentially a farm dog, the Dalmatian came late to intimate living with humans and seems to be trying to make up for it. It is long-suffering with clean habits, loyal and devoted, and gets very attached to children.

Appearance

One of the most elegant of breeds, this dog is tall and slim. The smooth, shiny coat with striking black or liver-coloured spots on a white background is a

This striking, good-looking dog, with its distinctive spots, makes a good and affectionate companion and family pet.

must know

There is some hip dysplasia in this breed. Deafness is also a worry but tests are available.

talking point wherever it goes. Dogs are 58–61cm (23–24in) in height; bitches are slightly smaller.

General care

With their working past, Dalmatians obviously want and need as much exercise as an owner can give. Undoubtedly, they should live in the country. Little grooming is required; a weekly brushing will suffice.

want to know more?

• The Kennel Club's comprehensive guide to *Breed Standards* is one of the best sources of information on utility group dog breeds
• You can Google the individual breed clubs on the Internet

6 Pastoral and working dogs

These groups include many of the guarding and herding breeds of dog. Since antiquity, dogs have been bred for their protective instincts, especially to guard livestock against predators. The pastoral group includes two styles of sheepdog: the British type, which is taught to work closely with a flock and take out single sheep or small groups; and the European style, which move sheep but are protective dogs. Corgis work with cattle while other breeds are all-purpose farm dogs. The working group contains mountain dogs, mastiffs and powerful guard dogs like the Rottweiler and Dobermann. Although they make good family pets, many of these breeds need firm handling and good socialization.

German Shepherd Dog

One of the most popular breeds in the world today, the German Shepherd Dog makes a loyal and affectionate family pet as well as an outstanding working dog. Highly intelligent, alert and very responsive, it is an extremely biddable dog and always a pleasure to own when it has been properly socialized and trained.

must know

There are several genetic anomalies: hip dysplasia, haemophilia (males), elbow dysplasia and digestive problems. Only buy puppies from breeders who test their breeding stock.

History

This breed was produced from an amalgam of North European herding breeds. The prototype has existed in Germany for many centuries – Tacitus, the Roman historian, mentioned the 'wolf like dog of the Rhineland'. In the nineteenth century, the German army officer Rittmeister von Stephanitz recognized the potential of this breed and he created the *Verein für Deutsche Schäfehunde* in order to control its development.

German Shepherd puppies need firm but kind handling and good socialization with people and other dogs, so they grow up into well-behaved, friendly adults.

Work

Arguably the greatest all-round working dog of all time, the German Shepherd Dog is an invaluable and fearless police dog worldwide, as well as a tracker dog, a guide dog for the blind, an assistance dog for the disabled and a patrol dog for security companies. It is extensively used as a search and rescue dog in mountains, avalanches, earthquakes and other emergencies.

Temperament

The German Shepherd Dog is intelligent, versatile and steady, whether as a pet in the home or as a working security dog. When properly socialized, no breed is more caring or loyal to its human family. It is easily trained to a high standard but it does need firm and kind handling.

This puppy's coat is fine and downy but it will get harsher and thicker and change colour as it grows.

Appearance

This is a big dog which is long in comparison to its
height. Powerful and muscular, it has a deep chest
and strong hindquarters. Its weather-resistant coat
consists of harsh outer guard hairs about 5cm (2in)
long with a thick undercoat. There is also a long-
coated variety which, although popular, cannot be
shown in the show ring. Colours include black with
tan, or gold to light grey. All black or all grey dogs
with light or brown markings are known as Sables.
White dogs are becoming more popular but they
cannot be shown and some are susceptible to
health problems, including deafness.

The German Shepherd's conformation gives it a
far-reaching, enduring movement and an elegant
head carriage. The pricked ears and bright eyes
create an alert and intelligent expression. Dogs are
63cm (25in) in height while bitches are slightly
smaller at 58cm (23in).

General care

This intelligent dog requires a lot of exercise and
mental stimulation, especially games. It has a
tendency to be quite vocal and to bark a lot as well
as its natural instincts to herd and guard, so you
must ensure that you control the games you play
with your dog and prevent it getting over-excited.
Your dog will be anxious to please and win your
praise, so reward any good behaviour as this breed
tends to be extremely sensitive to an owner's mood.

Socialization classes are essential for German
Shepherd Dog puppies, so they can learn to play
and interact with other dogs in a non-aggressive
way as they have a tendency towards dominance.

This dog excels at Obedience and Agility training and will enjoy the exercise and mental stimulation involved, working as a team with its owner. Because it is so active, however, it does need a high-quality, nutritious diet in order to stay healthy. At the same time, be careful not to over-feed your dog as it is a natural athlete. Regular walks each day on a lead, free running and playing games will all help to keep your dog fit and slim in optimum health.

Short-coated dogs need minimal grooming: just a good combing followed by a brushing twice weekly will rid the coat of dead hairs and keep it in good condition, especially in the moulting season. Finish the grooming session by shining the coat with a hound glove or a soft brush. Long-coated dogs will need to be groomed more regularly, especially after exercise if they get muddy or pick up dirt and debris. Pay special attention to the tail and paws.

German Shepherd Dogs are one of the breeds that are susceptible to hip dysplasia. When you buy a puppy, check the score for both hips.

must know

Potential buyers must be aware of the pitfalls. Because of its extreme popularity, this dog is subject to over-breeding. Many are bred by puppy farmers whose sole concern is making money. The nett result is that genetic anomalies are maintained and can stay with the breed. Deal only with breeders who have a proven record of testing their breeding stock with the current KC/BVA schemes. Have a vet examine your choice as soon as possible.

Border Collie

The most enthusiastic of all the working farm dogs, working cows and sheep with equal facility, the Border Collie has also become very popular as a family pet. Some find the time to be show dogs, and they excel in Obedience, Agility and Flyball.

must know

There is some low-level hip dysplasia in this breed. Genetic eye problems are being controlled but buy from tested parents and get the puppy tested at an appropriate time. There is also some deafness.

History

Sheepdogs have been a vital part of the shepherd's equipment since man first domesticated farm animals; without them the vast flocks of millions of sheep just would not exist. Undoubtedly, there were sheepdogs working flocks in Scotland long before the Romans invaded England, bringing with them their own breed of sheep and probably their own sheepdogs. They were interbred with the native dogs and the long process of evolution of the five Sheepdog breeds began. Shepherds are naturally secretive and nobody knows which breeds went into making the Border Collie, although some say the Newfoundland and the Borzoi. Queen Victoria fell for the Collie on her visits to Balmoral and under her patronage they prospered.

The watchful and inquisitive Border Collie is always alert and responsive.

Temperament

Anxious to please, highly intelligent and easily trained, the Border Collie is a sensitive dog and is inclined to be headstrong. It cares deeply for its family, especially children, and is an excellent guard dog.

Appearance

The Border Collie is medium-sized with a fairly long body. It comes in two different coats: smooth and moderately long. Any coat colour is permissible, including blue, but not too much white. Dogs are 53cm (21in) in height, while bitches are slightly less.

General care

This dog needs a huge amount of running exercise and things to occupy its mind. The smooth-coated variety only needs a weekly brush, but the longer coat requires combing every other day.

must know

Strangers ✓✓✓
Suspicious; will defend family and territory

Temperament ✓✓✓
Very affectionate but energetic family dog

Exercise ✓✓✓✓
Needs a great deal and mental stimulation.

Grooming ✓✓✓
Minimal for smooth; long coats need more

Other dogs ✓✓✓
Non-aggressive dog but likes to herd little dogs

Summary
Ideal for active owners

The Border Collie's superb herding ability makes it the most popular of all the working sheepdogs.

Old English Sheepdog

Not old by canine standards, this dog breed has been known for about 200 years, and it is now the most famous sheepdog of all, due to the paint advertising campaigns which featured it.

History

This dog is probably a relative of the Bearded Collie mixed with the Russian Owtcharka and other European and Asiatic breeds. At one time, there was a need for a strong, fierce dog to protect flocks of sheep from wolves. When these predators were brought under control, Old English Sheepdogs, or Bobtails as they are familiarly known, were an ideal cattle drover's dog – hard working, intelligent and healthy. With the advent of the railways, droving became superfluous and this breed became more of a companion dog, although a few stayed on the farms as general livestock workers. The first Old English Sheepdog club was formed in 1888 and the breed became a popular showdog.

Temperament

Always reliable and even-tempered, this handsome dog is non-aggressive, exuberant and full of fun. Although it is fond of children, it is too boisterous to be left alone with small ones. It likes to be close to its family and is very affectionate.

Appearance

The huge coat is what differentiates this large dog from all others. It has a very thick undercoat with profuse grey/blue guard hairs on the body and

The Old English Sheepdog has a profuse harsh-textured topcoat and waterproof undercoat.

Whereas show dogs have well covered heads, so it is difficult to see their eyes, it is customary for many pet dogs to be trimmed, making everyday care and grooming easier for owners.

white on the head and shoulders. In height, dogs are 61cm (24in) and upwards, while bitches are 56cm (22in) and upwards.

General care

Underneath the heavy coat is a strong, intelligent dog which needs long walks, exercise and doggie things to do. They are not too difficult to train and prefer to be active, particularly enjoying Agility. Due to their hard-working rural past, they are hardy dogs and easy to feed. The problem for owners is maintaining the coat as it requires time and dedication and should be deep combed every day to remove any debris which will start tangles, leading to matting. The ears and bottom should be cleaned on a routine basis. If this is too much work for you, the dog's coat can be shorn three times a year.

must know

Strangers ✓
Good guard dog, very watchful

Temperament ✓✓✓✓
Biddable, intelligent and easily trained

Exercise ✓✓✓✓
As much exercise as you can give

Grooming ✓✓✓✓✓
Important to groom every day

Other dogs ✓✓✓
Generally a friendly dog

Summary
An affectionate dog who needs a lot of attention

Shetland Sheepdog

Shetland is a windswept island located off the north coast of Scotland, and its cold, bleak aspect produces miniature livestock – Shetland ponies, cows and sheep – so it is natural that the dog used to control them is also small. Shetland Sheepdogs are now popular family pets as well as working dogs.

must know

Some hip dysplasia and eye anomalies are present in this breed. Puppies should be bought from tested parents and should themselves be tested.

History

Collie-type dogs were always present on the island of Shetland, but they were subsequently crossed with dogs from visiting whalers or fishermen from Scandinavia and Holland. A visit from Queen Victoria cruising the waters probably introduced crosses with the King Charles Spaniel, producing colours unknown in Collies. The Sheltie's standard work was to assist the shepherd in all his duties, protecting its charges by keeping them from the edge of cliffs and running back to warn its owner of approaching trouble.

Temperament

The Shetland Sheepdog has a sweet nature, always wanting to please and invariably willing. This is a one-man dog with a liking for outdoor activities. Even freezing cold, snow and appalling weather conditions do not worry this tough breed. A naturally clean dog, the Sheltie is very intelligent and easily trained, gentle and responsive, caring deeply for its family.

The perky little Shetland Sheepdog has an easily recognizable and abundant ruff of long, straight hair around its neck.

Appearance

The Sheltie is a very pretty, perky little dog with an abundant double coat – a harsh-textured outer coat and a soft, dense undercoat. It comes in brilliant colours, ranging from gold to mahogany, tri-colours, blue merle and black and white. Dogs are 37cm (14.5in) high while bitches are slightly smaller.

General care

A tireless breed, this dog will take all the walking its owner can give. In urban situations, it should have frequent walks, free running and play. The coat needs weekly attention: deep brushing with a radial nylon brush is recommended and knots behind the ears are a problem. The feet, hind legs and the fur under the tail should be trimmed with sharp scissors.

Alert and tireless, the Shetland Sheepdog is among the world's most popular dog breeds.

must know

Strangers ✓✓✓✓
Suspicious, will warn vociferously

Temperament ✓✓✓✓✓
Responsive, amicable nature

Exercise ✓✓✓✓
When adult, as much exercise as possible

Grooming ✓✓✓
Important to groom every week

Other dogs ✓✓✓
A friendly dog

Summary
An affectionate dog suitable for a lively family

Corgi (Cardigan and Pembroke)

These two breeds of Corgi worked on the farms of West Wales for hundreds of generations. They were cattle dogs, moving the cattle by nipping their heels, as well as general workers, keeping the land and people's homes free from vermin.

must know

Strangers ✓✓✓✓
Both breeds are good guard dogs

Temperament ✓✓✓✓✓
Cardigan: laid back
Pembroke: mischievous
Both good with children but must be socialized

Exercise ✓✓✓✓
Walks at least twice daily, garden games

Grooming ✓
Once a week, more when moulting

Other dogs ✓✓
Cardigan: friendly but dislikes being hustled
Pembroke: anxious to be friendly

Summary
Both breeds are loyal, affectionate family pets

History

Nothing much is known of their early history, as they lived on remote mountain farms and were virtually unknown outside these areas. The Welsh canine bibliographer Clifford Hubbard theorized that both breeds had the same origins but evolved differently. The Cardigan Corgi is the original Welsh cattle dog which remained in the relative obscurity of central Wales. The Pembroke Corgi began as the original Welsh Cattle dog but was crossed with the Spitz-type Swedish Vallhund introduced by the Vikings. In the eleventh century, Flemish weavers settled around Haverford West and brought their tailless Schipperkes which interbred with the native breeds. It is not easy to trace early dog shows scheduling *Corgwn* (Corgis); they were classified as *Cwn Sodli* (Heeler dogs). They were exhibited as *Corgwn* in 1925, and in 1934 The Kennel Club registered them as two breeds. A few are still worked but most are show dogs and pets now.

Temperament

Both breeds have similar temperaments; they are busy dogs, always looking for something to do. They are good guard dogs, faithful, affectionate, intelligent and good with children.

Appearance

Low on the leg and long in the body, both the Corgi breeds have pricked ears but set slightly differently. The Pembroke has the foxier expression with a short tail; the Cardigan is slightly longer in body with a full tail. Any coat colour is permissible in the Cardigan, but Pembrokes are self coloured red, sable, fawn or black and tan, with some white markings permitted. In height, Cardigans are 30cm (12in) high at the shoulder; Pembrokes are 25.5–30cm (10–12in).

must know

Breeders report no known problems. PRA has been eradicated in Cardigans but a Kennel Club DNA test is available.

General care

These hardy, inquisitive little dogs are good feeders but they need plenty of exercise and things to do. They often excel at Obedience, Agility and Flyball. They need to be groomed at least once a week.

Corgis are busy little dogs, which need to be occupied. Bright and alert, they are good companions. This is the Pembroke Corgi.

Boxer

The Boxer is a German manufactured breed derived from the ancient Mastiff-style dog that accompanied the Roman legions across Europe. Like several other big breeds, it has, in its lineage, the blood of the Bullenbeiser – dogs bred for bull baiting.

must know

There is some hip dysplasia but serious heart problems exist. Buy only from reputable breeders who test their stock. There is also some deafness in white dogs.

Work

Once they are over the puppy stages, Boxers are easily trained for all manner of security work. The breed is used in Europe as a police dog where its muscular, hard body can stop a criminal in his tracks. Armed forces make use of its determination and confident attitude. The Boxer's aggressive appearance often warns off wrong-doers, but this dog is not a biter and its looks belie its soft nature.

Temperament

Bred to be a companion, guard and show dog, the Boxer's intelligence and brightness of spirit endear it to most nationalities. It is an alert house guard with a booming voice, but although it is suspicious of strangers it is never vicious. As a member of a family, the Boxer is truly a fun dog, very affectionate and loyal to the end.

Boxer puppies can be extremely energetic and exuberant. They are easily socialized and trained.

Appearance

This dog has a superb athletic body, rippling with muscles, on powerful legs with cat-like feet. It is of medium size with a short, glossy coat in fawn shades, from light to deer red, or distinct brindle stripes. White is allowed but not exceeding one-third of the base colour. Dogs are 57–63cm (22.5–25in) high whereas bitches are slightly smaller.

General care

The Boxer can be boisterous and exuberant and it should be trained kindly not to jump up on visitors or the people or children whom it loves. Natural athletes, all Boxers need plenty of lead walking, activity, free running and play. Minimal grooming is required: a weekly brushing will remove any dead hairs from the short coat, which should then be polished with a chamois leather or hound glove.

The powerful-looking Boxer's aggressive appearance belies its soft, affectionate nature.

must know

Strangers ✓✓✓
A serious guard

Temperament ✓✓✓
Good natured but boisterous without aggression

Exercise ✓✓✓✓
Must have plenty

Grooming ✓
Weekly brushing

Other dogs ✓✓✓
Easy going

Summary
The right dog for the right family

Dobermann

This handsome, athletic dog makes a superb family pet as well as a working dog. However, like all powerful dog breeds, it needs good socialization, effective obedience training and affection from puppyhood to make it a well-behaved, friendly adult which is safe with people, children and other dogs.

must know

There is low to average hip dysplasia in this breed. Buy from eye-tested parents and have the puppy eye tested, too. Von Willebrands disease, wobbler syndrome and torsion are also possible.

History

This breed was designed in the 1880s by Herr Louis Dobermann, a German tax collector. At a time when taxes were collected personally, he wanted an alert and fearless dog with stamina to defend him as he travelled around on horseback. His secondary job as a 'dog catcher' gave him the opportunity to study various breeds. The Rottweiler, old German Pinscher and Manchester Terrier were probably the breed's foundation. Later on, it may have been refined with Pointer and Greyhound blood.

Work

Highly regarded as a guard and security dog, the Dobermann is much favoured by many security companies moving large sums of money. It was a watchdog and messenger in battles during World War II, and is now used by the police and military because of its intelligence, alertness and courage, to say nothing of its athletic strength.

Temperament

A devoted, affectionate house dog, the Dobermann is very intelligent and easily trained but its power must be kept under control. It is a devout family

If well socialized and trained, a puppy can adapt to family life.

companion which loves to be part of daily activities. Its guardianship of a family's children is legendary, but it must be trained firmly with kindness.

Appearance

The Dobermann is a big dog, most graceful with a refined outline. A powerhouse athlete, it may be a glossy black, brown, blue or fawn (Isabella) with rich tan, which must be well defined. Dogs are 69cm (27in) tall and bitches are 65cm (25.5in)

General care

An hour or so of walking every day with 10 minutes' free running will suffice. Add 15 minutes' play in the garden and a Dobermann will be happy and fit. Very little grooming is required; a weekly brush and polish with a chamoix leather will be enough.

must know

Strangers ✓✓✓✓✓
A powerful guard dog

Temperament ✓✓✓
A great family dog needing to be trained

Exercise ✓✓✓✓
An hour a day walking plus free running

Grooming ✓
A weekly brushing

Other dogs ✓✓✓
Seldom picks a fight but never backs down

Summary
A family dog for experienced owners

Powerful yet very elegant, the handsome Dobermann makes an affectionate family pet and show dog as well as a guard dog.

Great Dane

Although the Great Dane is classified as a working breed, it is many years since they were used as working dogs and now they are better known as family pets. However, these gentle giants do make good guard dogs and their size is intimidating to strangers.

must know

Strangers ✓✓✓✓
Suspicious nature, will guard owners

Temperament ✓✓✓✓
Friendly, outgoing, favours children

Exercise ✓✓✓✓
Puppies not too much; adults plenty

Grooming ✓
Minimal: weekly brush and polish with hound glove

Other dogs ✓✓✓✓
Gets on with others

Summary
A deeply affectionate big dog caring for its family

History

This dog's ancestors were giant war dogs from Asia Minor, probably originating from ancient Egypt. They were used as war dogs by Attila the Hun and fought against wild animals in Rome's Coliseum. Medieval pictures depict them in their fighting gear, consisting of an armoured coat with spikes. The modern Great Dane was developed in the 1500s in Germany for hunting wild boar. However, from 1882, when the Breed Club was formed, the breed changed course and became a pet and guard dog.

Temperament

This is a courageous, devoted but sensitive breed which belies its bloodthirsty past. Extremely family oriented, Great Danes are easily trained and very obedient. Although large, they are not clumsy and don't take up too much space. However, a big house and garden are best. Seriously fond of their family's children, they will defend them if danger threatens.

Appearance

The Great Dane is a majestic yet elegant dog with a soft expression and an athletic body with a look of 'dash and daring'. Colours range from brindle with stripes to fawn-light to dark, blue-light to dark slate, black or harlequin with black or blue patches which appear torn. Dogs are a minimum of 76cm (30in) in height while bitches are a minimum of 71cm (28in).

General care

These dogs need only gentle exercise when they are young and their bones are still growing. The amount of walking and running you give them can be built up gradually over time to develop their muscular athletic body. A fully-grown adult dog will demand plenty of walks and free running. Never play fight with this breed as you are unlikely to win and could get hurt. A weekly good brushing will keep the coat lustrous; the ears need cleaning at the same time.

In spite of its immense size and fighting past, the Great Dane is a gentle giant. Like many large breeds, its life expectancy is not long: only 10 years.

Mastiff

The Mastiff belongs to the general group known as *Molossus*, and while little is known of their absolute origins these powerful dogs have been around since written history began and were once used as guards, war dogs and fighting dogs.

must know

Strangers ✓✓✓
Suspicious, will warn vociferously

Temperament ✓✓✓✓✓
Easy going, affable, tolerates children happily

Exercise ✓✓✓
When adult, as much exercise as possible

Grooming ✓
Important to groom every week

Other dogs ✓✓

Does not seek altercation

Summary
A big softie needing love and involvement, very protective of family

History

This dog is thought to be the descendant of the Tibetan Mastiff, used by the Persians, Greeks and Egyptians as war dogs. The Roman armies spread the breed through Europe, assisted by Phoenician coastal traders. When Julius Caesar invaded Britain, he brought his own Mastiff-style war dogs (*Epirus Pugnaces*), which were beaten by the huge, aggressive British dogs (Cornish *Canis Pugnaces*). In 1066, the Norman William the Conqueror defeated the English in one day but it took two days to rid himself of the British war dogs. Used originally as a boar hunter and then for security, bull baiting and dog fighting, the breed slowly deteriorated and fell into disfavour until after World War II when there were only eight Mastiffs left in Britain. It was saved by imports from Canada and has since recovered in numbers.

Temperament

Despite its bloody history, the Mastiff is the most amiable dog – a gentle giant, calm, intelligent and extremely loyal. It has a great liking for children and will put up with their play with endless patience. This dog improves in character the closer it gets to its owners but care must be taken to train it and control its strength. As a guard, it has no peer.

Do not consider owning one of these huge dogs unless you have ample space and can afford to feed a high-quality diet.

Appearance

The Mastiff is heavy-boned with a large square head viewed from all angles and a short muzzle cut off square. It has a big chest and powerful body. The short, close coat may be apricot-fawn, silver-fawn or dark brown brindle. The muzzle, ears and nose are black with black around the eye orbits extending upwards. No height or weight for this great dog is quoted in the British standard.

General care

Puppies need quality food with a high-protein content and plenty of easy exercise, although no stress should be placed on joints until the bones have ossified at around two years old. Treat these dogs as athletes, and keep them slim and muscular. Give them something soft to sleep on – their weight can distort their elbows. Groom weekly with a stiff brush, cleaning the ears and the wrinkles.

must know

This breed suffers hip dysplasia and elbow dysplasia. Other genetic faults at low level exist; check with the breeder and The Kennel Club.

Rottweiler

This handsome, immensely powerful dog is popular as a family pet as well as a guard dog. Only experienced owners should consider owning this breed as it needs good obedience training, firm control and socialization to make it a good-mannered pet.

must know

A small amount of hip dysplasia is present. Osteochondrosis Dessicans (OCD) is largely under control, but Rottweilers may suffer from cruciate ligament rupture, entropion and eczema.

History

The Rottweiler's likely origin is from Mastiff-style dogs which travelled with Roman armies driving livestock as they swept northwards conquering Europe. First used as boar hunters, then as cattle drovers in the German city of Rotweill, they doubled as custodians of traders' money. This dog is devoted to its family but must be taught its place kindly and persistently. Because of its intensely protective nature, never leave it with young children as, like all guarding breeds, it might misinterpret signals.

Puppies need kind but firm handling and socialization if they are to grow up into good-natured adult dogs.

Work

Very few Rottweilers are now used for their droving ability. Instead, their strong protective instincts are used in security work, patrolling building sites and industrial installations and protecting security van guards. Because of their intelligence, some countries train them as customs and police dogs, mountain rescue dogs and even for sled hauling.

Temperament

Highly intelligent, the Rottweiler's strong naturally protective instincts need proper socialization with firm but kind training. Although generally good natured and biddable, these powerful dogs can be difficult in the wrong hands. They should never be left alone with children or strangers.

Appearance

A big, thick-set, muscled dog, the Rottweiler should show boldness and confidence, never nervousness or aggressiveness. A calm look indicates a good nature. It is very powerful with great strength and a broad chest. Dogs are 63–69cm (25–27in) in height while bitches are 58–63cm (23–25in).

General care

Keep these dogs' muscles hard with walking, free running and play. If living in a town, they should be taken out for a brisk walk at least twice a day. With their thick, smooth coat, they need only be brushed once a week with a stiff brush to remove dead hairs.

In spite of its powerful body and formidable appearance, this dog can make a good pet if it is socialized and trained properly.

must know

Strangers ✓✓✓✓
Great guard dog

Temperament ✓✓✓
Good natured but can be dominant without good training

Exercise ✓✓✓✓
Frequent, thrives on plenty of activity

Grooming ✓
Easy care; weekly brush and comb

Other dogs ✓✓✓✓
Take care as they will not back down

Summary
The time spent training pays dividends

St Bernard

This large, impressive-looking dog is thought by some to be a member of the *Molossus* group of dogs, used by ancient Greeks, Persians and Romans as war dogs, guards and fighting dogs. However, it is anything but aggressive and is very affectionate.

must know

Strangers ✓✓✓
Suspicious, will warn vociferously

Temperament ✓✓✓✓✓
Gentle ?????

Exercise ✓✓✓✓
When adult, as much exercise as possible

Grooming ✓✓✓✓
Twice a week

Other dogs ✓✓
Not given to quarrelling

Summary
A sensitive, very benign family dog, loyal and gentle

History

Roman armies took their war dogs marching north through the Alpine passes and these may have been the ancestors of the Alpine Mastiff-style breeds. Another theory is that some big 'cow herding' breeds were already in existence and the St Bernard evolved from them. Their name comes from the St Bernard pass between Switzerland and Italy where a hospice was founded in 1050 to aid travellers. In the mid-1600s, the hospice was under threat from brigands, so they acquired big watch dogs. They proved so successful in finding lost travellers and detecting incipient avalanches that the monks started to breed them. The first St Bernards had short, thick hair, but when they came to Britain in 1810 they were crossed with Newfoundlands to get longer hair, making them popular as pets but not so good in snow; they were first exhibited in 1863.

Temperament

This dog has an unsurpassed gentle temperament and seems to be 'in tune' with its human family, particularly children. Intelligent, courageous and faithful, the St Bernard is relatively easy to train but is very sensitive by nature, so harsh training is always counter-productive.

Appearance

This dog is well boned with a broad, muscled back. There are two coats: roughs (dense and flat with well feathered thighs and tail); and smooths (close and hound-like, with light feathering on the thighs and tail). Colours may be orange, mahogany-brindle, red-brindle, or white with patches of these colours. They can have a white muzzle, blaze, collar, chest, forelegs, feet and tail end, and black shading on the face and ears. The Standard gives no size but the 'taller the better' as long as symmetry is kept.

General care

Puppies and young dogs should not have long walks; wait until the bones and joints have ossified. Good, nourishing food is needed for rapid growth at this age. Keep this dog wormed at the correct intervals, as worms ruin the coat. Groom at least twice a week.

The gentle St Bernard requires a lot of space, grooming and attention from its owner. It will repay all the work you put in with outstanding loyalty and affection.

Siberian Husky

In their land of origin, Huskies are cherished working dogs. Used for hauling sleds, their strength and stamina allow them to make phenomenally long journeys. In the West, they are usually kept as companion dogs although sled dog racing is growing rapidly.

must know

Strangers ✓
Just not a guard dog, too easy-going

Temperament ✓✓✓✓
Kind gentle and affectionate

Exercise ✓✓✓✓✓
A glutton for running; try cart training

Grooming ✓✓✓✓✓
Bi-weekly deep grooming required

Other dogs ✓✓
Generally friendly, good disposition

Summary
An excellent companion for energetic families

History

Husky sled dogs were the only means of transport in Alaska during the gold rush of 1900. In 1920, a team of 20 Siberian Huskies pulled a sled 340 miles, carrying vaccines to the diphtheria-stricken city of Nome, saving the population. A statue of a sled dog located in Central Park, New York, celebrates that remarkable achievement.

Temperament

The Siberian Husky is gentle, friendly, intelligent and biddable. Because the breed lived closely, probably for thousands of years, with the Chukchi nation, they are

Elegant and athletic, the Siberian Husky does not bark but howls and talks instead.

'people orientated' dogs. Easy-going, easy to train and anxious to please their owners, Siberian Huskies are essentially pack dogs who understand and love their family, particularly children.

Appearance

This dog is very alert looking, medium sized and lithe with grace. It has an abundant weatherproof coat of which the undercoat is thick and soft. The breed comes in many different coat colours, and the facial colours can be contrasting, unusual and striking. Dogs are 53–60cm (21–24in) in height, whereas bitches are slightly smaller.

Siberian Huskies are energetic and friendly dogs. If they are not working, they need to be busy and you have to devote a lot of time to play and exercise.

General care

Without their work, Siberian Huskies need frequent running exercise to keep them both physically and mentally fit and healthy, and new owners should really consider joining a specialist club which races with wheeled carts. Do not own one unless you are fit and very energetic. These dogs moult freely and their double coat must be groomed by combing it at least twice a week, or the undercoat can knot.

7 Toy dogs

This group of small and miniature dogs contains many popular companion breeds, such as King Charles Spaniels, Pugs and Yorkshire Terriers. Many of the diminutive breeds were originally developed as lap dogs for royal and aristocratic women. Their size and friendly disposition make them suitable companions for elderly people and perfect pets for city life as they need less space and exercise than larger dogs. Their main role in life is to bring their human family affection, entertainment, friendship and warmth.

King Charles Spaniel

Under the name of 'Comforter', the dwarf spaniel has been appreciated by aristocracy in Britain and Europe since medieval times. It was first mentioned by Dr Caius in his book *De Canibus Britannicis*, published in 1570, the first dog book ever written.

These perky little dogs come in a range of colours, including ruby, the traditional Blenheim and tricolour, as well as black and tan.

History

Some people think the origin of this breed was in Japan, others in China. King Charles II supposedly imported his from Spain, but others were already in Britain which may have added to the evolution of the breed. He was besotted with his spaniels, which had the run of the Westminster Palace, annoying the diarist Samuel Pepys (1633–1703), who grumbled that the king was childlike, always playing with his dogs and rarely concerning himself with the affairs of state. Although they were basically companion dogs, there are records of them being used in the hunting field. The breed changed in size, shape and colour until Victorian times, and eventually four varieties emerged. Only two of them received Kennel Club status: the King Charles and the Cavalier King Charles. It is important to note that these breeds are separate and quite unlike each other in structure, the heads in particular being very different.

Temperament

One of the gentlest, kindest dogs, the King Charles Spaniel is a great friend to children of all ages and sensitive to its owner's moods. Highly intelligent and a quick learner, it makes a good family pet.

Appearance

This small cobby dog has a domed head, long ears and a soft silky coat with plenty of furnishings. Coat colours are: black and tan – pearly white base with even black patches and brilliant tan markings; Blenheim – pearly white base with chestnut patches, a white blaze with a chestnut 'thumb' print in the centre; and Ruby – whole coloured in rich ruby red, no white permissible. No height is given but its weight should be in the range 3.6–6.3kg (6–14lb). Importance is given to balance and symmetry.

General care

The furnishings must be kept clean or they tangle severely. The ears must be groomed and cleaned, and it's a good idea to feed from tall narrow containers which keep the ears out of the food. A couple of walks during the day with play in the garden will give sufficient exercise.

must know

Strangers ✓✓✓
Will warn and is watchful

Temperament ✓✓✓✓✓
Intelligent, gentle

Exercise ✓✓✓
Two walks daily and play

Grooming ✓✓✓
Pay attention to ears

Other dogs ✓✓✓✓✓
Non aggressive

Summary
Ideal family companion

Puppies are very appealing and are eager to please their owners. This makes them relatively easy to socialize and train.

Cavalier King Charles Spaniel

The Cavalier King Charles has become the most popular of the Toy Spaniels. It is the ideal small companion dog with lots of character. Affectionate and friendly, it loves to interact and play games with everyone within the family.

must know

Some hip dysplasia is present in this breed. Both sexes should be heart tested, as mitral valve disease and patus ductus arteriosis may be in some lines. Puppies and their parents should always undergo eye testing.

History

Today's King Charles Spaniel was almost certainly developed from the land spaniels of the fourteenth century which may have come originally from Spain. The Stuarts were besotted with them and named them 'King Charles'. Indeed, Charles II shared his bed with several. They went out of fashion in Britain when William of Orange reigned but later staged a comeback in the nineteenth century when a toy red and white spaniel was bred at Blenheim by the Duke of Marlborough. Although the breed started as a gundog and companion, it became a showdog and pet when dog shows started in the mid 1800s. A fashion developed for short-nosed dogs and the original breed began to decline again. An American, Roswell Eldridge, offered handsome prizes to anyone who could reverse the trend and, slowly, by selective breeding, today's type of longer-nosed Cavalier King Charles Spaniel evolved.

Temperament

Docile, gentle and intelligent, the Cavalier King Charles quickly learns the ways of its human family. With its friendly character, it is a joy to own. A fun dog, it has confidence and can be gently assertive. It loves to play with children but not roughly.

Appearance

This is an elegant, refined small dog with a kind expression and an out-going perky character, displaying a free action when moving. It has a silky coat with colours that are vivid and clearly delineated. Dogs are 30–33cm (12–13in) in height.

General care

Being small, this dog needs less exercise than the bigger spaniels. However, it's keen on activity of all kinds, particularly play. The silky coat needs weekly combing with attention paid to any tangles in the feathering and ears, especially after walks.

The head of the Cavalier King Charles is totally different from that of the King Charles Spaniel (see pages 166–167).

Yorkshire Terrier

The Yorkshire Terrier makes a perfect house pet, particularly for the elderly, as it eats only a tiny amount of food and takes up very little space. Its acute hearing picks up strangers in the vicinity and, although it's not a yappy dog, it will let you know they're there.

Even show dogs with their silky, glamorous coats are spirited.

History

In the early nineteenth century, coal mines were ridden with rats and some miners in northern England developed a terrier that was small enough to carry in their pockets when they went down the mines. Starving workers came south from Scotland, seeking work, with their rough terriers, the Skye and Clydesdale Terriers. These were subsequently inter-bred with the Old English Broken-haired and Manchester Terriers to produce the now familiar Yorkshire Terrier.

When dog showing began around 1850, the dog breeders realized that pretty little companion dogs were worth more money and therefore refined the terrier, producing today's dog.

Temperament

This little dog will give you unlimited affection, but because it has a strong independent streak, its early socialization and training will need patience and kindness. Under the gentle looks and loving nature lurks some of the feistiness inherited from its rough working dog ancestry. It will still hunt mice and rats but at home is full of fun and mischief. Children need to be gentle as the Yorkie is very small and can easily get hurt in rough games.

Appearance

The Yorkshire Terrier is an elegant, tiny dog with a spectacular flowing coat, which is long and silky and of a distinctive steel blue colour with a rich golden tan on the head, chest and legs. Dogs are 25cm (10in) or less in height, and can weigh up to 3.1kg (7lb).

General care

Yorkshire Terriers are inquisitive and sociable dogs and they love going out. They will need a long walk or at least a stroll once round the block twice daily. Sniffing around the garden and play hunting are an equal joy to them. Because of the length and texture of their coat, it does have a tendency to tangle and matt easily, so a daily gentle combing session is essential for this breed. If you don't have the time or the inclination to groom your dog every day, keep the coat cut short (as shown below).

must know

Strangers ✓✓✓
Suspicious; will bark a warning

Temperament ✓✓✓✓✓
Fun, mischievous, loving

Exercise ✓✓
A little or a lot

Grooming ✓✓✓✓✓
Very important: daily brushing and combing are essential

Other dogs ✓✓✓
No great problems

Summary ✓✓✓✓✓
A great pet for old and young alike

When buying a puppy, always make sure that you see them with their mother and observe them closely to ascertain which has the best temperament.

When grooming any Yorkie, it is important to comb the long hair on the dog's head, gently teasing out any knots and tangles.

Gently comb and then trim the hair at the sides of the head as well as the beard under the chin.

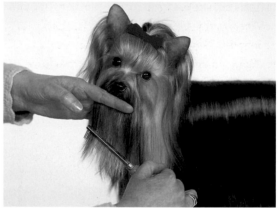

Comb the coat all over to keep it silky and tangle-free. Then gently brush the long hair to keep the coat straight all over.

Grooming

The Yorkshire Terrier is one of the world's great show dog breeds and presentation, grooming and coat condition are of great importance if you are planning to show your dog one day. However, even pet Yorkies need regular grooming if you keep their coat long and natural.

The two most important steps for maintainin a superb show coat are daily oiling to soften the hair and prevent any splits, and putting it in special paper 'crackers' to keep the show coat straight. The crackers are applied gently to the topknot, mouth hair, beard and other parts of the body. They must be introduced gradually so that the dog gets used to wearing them. Be gentle or the dog may never accept the procedure. Of course, this takes a lot of time and patience for both the owner and the dog.

Apply the paper crackers gently to show dogs. Get an experienced person to show you how to do this. You can go to special classes to learn how to prepare a dog.

This Yorkshire Terrier has a long, silky coat which is straight and in optimum condition.

Pekingese

This is truly one of the most ancient companion breeds in the world. The Pekingese is a good example of a dog designed for no other reason than to serve humanity. According to legend, it evolved from interbreeding between a lion and a monkey, and hence its leonine appearance and sharp intelligence.

must know

Strangers ✓✓✓
Friendly but will bark

Temperament ✓✓✓✓
Intelligent fun dog who believes itself to be big

Exercise ✓✓
Walks twice daily

Grooming ✓✓✓
Important to groom every day

Other dogs ✓✓✓
Excellent with own breed, may try to dominate others

Summary
An affectionate, fun companion

History

Myths surrounding the Pekingese go back many centuries and they are mentioned in the annals of the Yuan dynasty (1206–1333). Pekes featured in the art of the Ming dynasty beginning 1368 and were the favourites of Chinese rulers right through into the twentieth century. The existence of these dogs and how they were bred was always a closely guarded secret in China which was jealously kept from the Western world.

After the war between China and the West in 1856, the Imperial Palace was looted and several dogs were removed by British navy and army personnel and later brought back to Britain. One was given to Queen Victoria and the remainder to the British aristocracy. A few dogs were bred and exhibited, and in 1904 a club was formed and the breed increased in popularity.

Temperament

An intelligent little dog, the Pekingese is full of fun and is relatively easy to train. It has great dignity, is afraid of nothing on four legs and genuinely believes that it is a big dog. It loves attention and being part of the family's activities.

Appearance

This handsome little dog is so small that its huge double coat makes it stand out from all others. All coat colours are allowed except albino and liver. No height is given but dogs should weigh 5kg (11lb).

General care

Owners must be prepared to devote time to the maintenance of the coat which is described as 'the breed's crowning glory'. A thorough combing and brushing daily is of utmost importance, as the presence of any detritus can be the cause of tangles and matting and removing them can cause hair loss. Inspecting the ears, eyes, teeth and rear end is also necessary. A couple of daily walks are all that's needed, but they should be augmented with play in the garden to stimulate this active dog's mind. Good nourishing food is a strict requirement for coat growth but the dog must not be allowed to get fat.

The Peke's billowing coat looks fabulous but will need daily grooming to keep it tangle free and in excellent condition.

Pug

Pugs are endearing characters and make excellent and loving companions. They enjoy human company and living in a family pack. The breed standard's description of 'multum in parvum' is extremely apt as you get a lot of personality in a little dog.

must know

Generally, the Pug enjoys good health but sometimes experiences a little difficulty in breathing, so take care in hot weather. Their protuberant eyes are vulnerable to scratches, so take care of them.

History

The Pug and Pekingese may have been originally related because of the striking similarity of their muzzles and body shape. However, they were separate breeds by the 1600s, as shown in Chinese art. Dutch mariners brought them to Holland whereupon they became favourites of royalty after a pet Pug warned William, Prince of Orange, that Spanish soldiers were approaching to capture him at the battle of Hermingny and he escaped. William and Mary introduced the Pug to Britain where it was often decorated with orange ribbons as an

Pugs have forceful characters and are very strong-willed.

With its distinctive black face and prominent eyes, the Pug makes a rewarding and entertaining pet dog.

honoured member of the Royal Household of Orange. There is no evidence that this breed ever worked although, from an evolutionary point of view, they are Mastiffs. Their 'work' has always been to bring solace to human beings for whom they have an uncanny understanding.

Temperament

Tolerant and easy-going with children, Pugs are very intelligent with an independent comical character. They are guaranteed to bring laughter into any household with their strange facial expressions. They like sitting up high to watch the world go by. They are stubborn but easily trained to be clean.

Appearance

The Pug is a sturdy, thick-set small dog with flat features and a distinctive curled tail. It has a fine, smooth, short coat, which may be coloured silver, apricot, fawn or black with a black facial mask. It is 25–28cm (10–11in) in height.

General care

Pugs do not require excessive walking but enjoy a walk twice a day as they like seeing the world. Grooming is easy – a light brushing daily gives a glow to a Pug's coat. Make sure you keep the eyes, ears and crease above the nose clean.

must know

Strangers ✓✓✓
Not a guard dog but will warn of strangers

Temperament ✓✓✓✓
Even tempered and lively, humorous

Exercise ✓✓✓
Regular exercise but not excessive

Grooming ✓
A light brushing daily

Other dogs ✓✓✓
No problems

Summary
A great companion if you don't mind a little snoring

Pomeranian

This pretty little dog is unusually confident for its size and often unfazed by larger breeds. The Pomeranian has a big personality and loves to play games and be involved in everything.

History

A type of tiny Spitz dog is depicted on Roman artefacts and there is evidence of its existence throughout Europe ever since. However, almost certainly the close relations of this minuscule dog are the much larger Nordic Spitz breeds, such as the Samoyed and Keeshond. It came to Britain from Pomerania, Germany, around 1870 in the form of the much bigger German Spitz, weighing 13.6kg (30lb). The British bred them much smaller and gave them their new name, and by 1896 they were down to 3.6kg (8lb). However, they did not become popular until Queen Victoria exhibited her own dog at The Kennel Club's show after which the breed's future was assured.

Temperament

The Pomeranian is a happy and amusing little dog which is very fond of its family and given to being noisy unless it is trained otherwise. Full of vitality, energy and fun, Pomeranians are always anxious to involve themselves in family activities. However, they are docile with children who must take care not to be rough as the Pom's bones are very small and can get damaged easily.

A wide range of coat colours is permissible for the Pomeranian, including cream, sable, white, brown, red and orange.

Happy and vivacious, Pomeranians are good companions and fun dogs to own. They love to play games with their human family.

Appearance

This is a Lilliputian dog, a tiny round ball of fluff. The adult coat is abundant, thick and plush. All colours are permissible, including whole colours – white, black, brown, pale blue or vivid orange – and parti-coloured. Dogs weigh 1.8–2kg (4–4.5lb) whereas bitches are in the range 2–2.5kg (4.5–5.5lb).

General care

Running and playing in the garden is sufficient exercise for many Poms but they do enjoy an outing. Brush the coat deeply on a daily basis to prevent knotting and tangles, which form due to the plush thickness.

Poms have a large distinctive Spitz-type ruff of fur.

Bichon Frise

This elegant little dog has an affectionate nature and bonds very strongly with its owner. Although small, the Bichon Frise is very spirited and loves to play games. It is an ideal canine companion with an undiminished ability to perform tricks.

must know

There are some eye problems under investigation within this breed. Legge Perthes disease and slipping patella also exist.

History

This is a breed of antiquity stemming from the Barbet of the Mediterranean region from which four breeds emerged: the Bichon Maltaise, Bichon Bolognese, Bichon Havanese and Bichon Teneriffe. The latter breed was adopted by fourteenth-century Italian and Spanish nobility and thence the French court. King Henri III (1547–1589) was so enamoured of them that he carried them in baskets attached to ribbons round his neck. However, the breed went out of favour in the late 1800s, reverting to 'commoner' status and was extensively used by circus performers and street musicians due to their lively intelligence. Eventually recognized by the French in 1934, it was given its name, *Bichon à Poil Frise*, or 'Bichon of the Curly Coat'.

Bichon Frise puppies are very vivacious and love to play games.

Temperament

This little dog has a lively, kind nature and is extremely faithful, following its favourite person like a white shadow. A happy, friendly breed without vices, the Bichon Frise is boisterous with a sense of humour, quick to learn and inventive.

Appearance

This is a small dog with silky, corkscrewing curls, which are always white in colour. When trimmed correctly, the Bichon has a rounded aspect with the black of the eyes and nose contrasting vividly. Ideally, dogs are 23-28cm (9-11in) in height.

General care

Because of their enthusiasm, these dogs do need plenty of walks and things to do, such as interactive play in the garden. Their coat must have attention on a daily basis, otherwise it tangles and knots easily and may smell. If wished, however, it can be kept short in a 'puppy cut'.

Bichons should have a black nose and really dark, round eyes.

Chihuahua

Totally unaware of their diminutive size, Chihuahuas really do believe themselves to be Mastiffs in heavy disguise. However, these feisty little dogs make extremely loyal pets and they enjoy family life and human company.

must know

This breed can suffer from slipping patella and some heart murmurs.

History

Experts are baffled as to the real origins of this tiny dog. Americans discovered the breed in Chihuahua State, Mexico, and thought it was Mexican, but there is no evidence to support this. Some believe the ancient Toltecs bred them, others that they were sacred dogs of the Aztecs but, again, there is no evidence. Interestingly, some European breeds resemble them closely, especially the Portuguese Podengo and the Maltese Kelb Ta But (pocket dog). In 1519, the Spanish Conquistador Cortes conquered the Aztecs and it may be the case that his forces took little companion dogs with them, who became the ancestors of the modern-day Chihuahua.

The long-haired Chihuahua will need regular grooming twice a week to keep the coat looking good with a soft texture.

The smooth-haired Chihuahua is a dainty little dog. Affectionate and bright, it makes the perfect companion and family pet.

Temperament

Intelligent and easy to live with, Chihuahuas' only work is to be amusing companions. Most people keep more than one as they live together easily and share their home with cats and other pets. Care must be exercised when children handle them as their bones are so small. They adore being fussed over.

Appearance

Tiny, dainty and active, Chihuahuas may be smooth-coated or long-haired in any colour or mixture. It can weigh up to 2.7kg (6lb) although the preferred weight is in the range 1–1.8kg (2–4lb).

General care

The smooth-coated variety needs minimal grooming, but the long-haired variety should be brushed and combed lightly twice weekly. Active and athletic, the Chihuahua does not need excessive exercise but it loves a walk and to play in the garden.

Maltese

The exquisite little Maltese is another breed whose roots have been lost in antiquity and go back to pre-Christian times around the Mediterranean area. Its long, flowing, luxurious coat is pure white, making it a very glamorous-looking companion dog.

must know

Strangers ✓✓✓
Will bark but is then friendly

Temperament ✓✓✓✓✓
Happy nature, vigorous, sensitive, fun loving

Exercise ✓✓✓
Not much: a little stroll twice daily and play in the garden

Grooming ✓✓✓✓
Full coat: a daily chore. Cut down pet coat: daily brush and comb

Other dogs ✓✓✓✓
Very good

Summary
Devoted, loves family involvement, humorous

History

Similar dogs have been known since the fourteenth century BC in Egypt; an effigy appears on the tomb of Rameses II. They were also in ancient Greece and probably travelled to Malta and Sicily with the Romans. It is said that they brought the breed to Britain but there is no real evidence. Known in Britain since 1500,

The long, silky, straight, pure white coat is the crowning glory of the diminutive Maltese.

they became favourites of court ladies who used them as living hot water bottles and personal flea catchers. They were first exhibited in 1859 and have become popular all-round pets and show dogs.

Temperament

This dog has a very loving nature, adores its owners and expects to be adored in return. Training is not difficult but they are so sensitive that, if upset, they will do nothing. They are vigorous and full of fun, enjoying games, but they can be a bit yappy. They are very good with children who must be taught to be careful so as not to injure their pet accidentally.

Appearance

This short-legged dog is fairly long in the body whose mark of distinction is the long, pure white, silky coat; in the show dog the coat can trail on the floor. In height, both sexes are 25.5cm (10in).

General care

The small Maltese does not need a lot of exercise; a walk twice a day is generally sufficient. If you have a garden it will run about to exercise itself. The small amount of food must be of high quality to preserve the texture and condition of the coat, which must be combed every day. Not to do so creates tangles which, when removed, will leave holes. You need real commitment to maintain a show coat. It will require frequent washing with a dog shampoo and the hair preserved with curlers (crackers). It is not practical to keep a pet in a show coat, so it is usually cut about 2.5cm (1in) from the floor in a ballerina cut but still needs grooming every day.

Papillon

The Papillon (Butterfly dog) is yet another breed whose ancestry is lost. This is probably because those responsible for breeding it were illiterate or recording it was not considered important.

must know

Strangers ✓✓✓✓
Barks but then friendly

Temperament ✓✓✓✓✓
Very lively, affectionate, loves close contact with its owner

Exercise ✓✓✓✓
Plenty of garden games and short daily walks; when fit will walk miles

Grooming ✓✓
Light brush and comb daily. Care of ear and coat fringes important

Other dogs ✓✓✓✓
No problems

Summary
Happy, amusing, faithful but likes to rule

History

Belgium, France and Spain all claim the Papillon as theirs although a terra cotta statue of the breed was discovered in a second-century Roman tomb in Belgium. There was silence until a drop-eared breed, known as a Phalene (meaning 'moth'), of similar bodily appearance was depicted in paintings and frescoes dating from the thirteenth and fourteenth centuries in Italy. What led to the erect ears of the Papillon, the Butterfly dog, is not known, but they may have been the result of an outcross mating or a genetic mutation. After the fourteenth century it was only a short time before this pretty little dog became a great favourite in all

The stylish Papillon is instantly recognizable with its long bat-like ears, resembling the wings of a butterfly - and hence its name.

the royal courts of Western Europe. Today Papillons are popular show dogs with more exhibits at Crufts than any other Toy breed.

Temperament

This is a lively, adaptable breed, which is extremely affectionate and easy to train. Papillons thrive in the close contact of their owners and they make excellent house dogs, barking very loudly at the approach of any strangers. Totally unafraid, they will defend their home and family.

Appearance

This is a dainty looking dog which belies the fact that it is strong and resilient. The ears are likened to butterflies, the distinctive feature which makes them different from all other breeds. They are large – almost bat-like – and facing forward with long fringes of hair. The coat is abundant, flowing with long silky hair. the colour is always white with patches of any colour except liver. Dogs are 20–38cm (8–11in) high but they should appear slightly longer when they are properly furnished with a ruff and hind fringes.

General care

The breed may not look robust but these dogs are surprisingly normal and should be treated like any other small dog. Papillons like to play but children must be trained not to be rough with them because their bones are small. Food presents no problems, but care should be taken not to over-feed. The soft coat and fringes are a feature of the breed and should be groomed carefully every day to prevent tangles.

must know

Patella luxation and small eye problems are being investigated by The Kennel Club.

want to know more?

• For information on the Toy breeds, consult The Kennel Club's book on *Breed Standards*

Need to know more?

Organizations

British Veterinary Association
9 Mansfield Street
London W1M 0AT

The Kennel Club
1–5 Clarges Street
Piccadilly
London W1J 8AB
tel: 0870 606 6750
fax: 020 7518 1058
www.thekennelclub.org.uk

Hound Group

Hound group
tel: 01527 871061
Basset Hound Club
tel: 01892 531156
Bloodhound Club
tel: 01458 878800
Greyhound Club
tel: 01706 524993
Irish Wolfhound Club
tel: 01302 722166
National Whippet Association
tel: 01268 288091
Norwegian Elkhound Association of Great Britain
tel: 01563 540194
Rhodesian Ridgeback Club of Great Britain
tel: 01270 666215

Gundog Group

Brittany Club of Great Britain
tel: 01621 817728
Flat Coated Retriever Society
tel: 01162 793203
English Setter Club
tel: 01446 772973
German Shorthaired Pointer Club
tel: 01581 400253
Irish Setter Association
tel: 01553 840966
Italian Spinone Club of Great Britain
tel: 0870874 3082
Labrador Retriever Club
www.thelabradorretriever club.com
Pointer Club
tel: 01865 343435
Weimaraner Club of Great Britain
tel: 01799 523605

Terrier Group

Airedale (National Association)
tel: 01993 881185
Border Terrier Club
tel: 0191371 9405
Bull Terrier Club
tel: 01858 432610
Bull Terrier (Mini)
tel: 029 2079 1658

Cairn Terrier Club
tel: 01259 781438
Fox Terrier (Smooth) Association
tel: 01286 881344
Fox Terrier (Wire) Association
tel: 01732 222248
Kerry Blue Association of England
tel: 01787 269977
Norfolk Terrier Club of Great Britain
tel: 01666 841197
Norwich Terrier Club
tel: 01708 473897
Parson Russell Terrier
tel: 01905 821440
Staffordshire Bull Terrier Club
tel: 01299 403382
Welsh Terrier Club
tel: 01515467516
West Highland White Terrier Club
tel: 01963 440493

Utility Group

Boston Terrier Club
tel: 01892 652095
British Bulldog Club
tel: 01400 282163
British Dalmatian Club
tel: 01543 490849
Lhasa Apso Club
tel: 01603 868280

Mini Schnauzer Club
tel: 01785 760557
Poodle Club
tel: 020 8500 2335
Schnauzer Club of Great Britain
tel: 01235 851952
Shih Tzu Club
tel: 01666 822 480

Pastoral and Working Groups

Border Collie Club of Great Britain
tel: 0161 485 4544
British Association of German Shepherd Dogs
tel: 0121 353 9872
English Shetland Sheep Dog Club
tel: 01285 659449
Old English Sheepdog Club
tel: 01793 741002
Welsh Corgi Association (Cardigan)
tel: 01788 812156
Welsh Corgi Club
tel: 01633 875554
British Boxer Club
tel: 01235 835207
British Rottweiler Association
tel: 01953 600602
Dobermann Club
tel: 01205 821583

English St Bernard Club
tel: 01666 510295
Great Dane Club
tel: 01787 237 969
Mastiff Association
tel: 01464 871253
Newfoundland Club
tel: 01502 476609
Siberian Husky Club of Great Britain
tel: 0871 277 6783

Toy Group

United Kingdom Toy Dog Society
tel: 0151 486 3570
Bichon Frise of Great Britain
tel: 01323 843947
British Chihuahua Club
tel: 01249 821848
British Pekingese Club
tel: 01777 838383
Cavalier King Charles Spaniel Club
tel: 01390 430554
King Charles Spaniel Association
tel: 01934 822758
Maltese Club
tel: 01276 857786
Papillon (Butterfly Dog) Club
tel: 01543 256394
Pekingese (British Club)
tel: 01777 838383

Pomeranian Club
tel: 01453 821739
Pug Dog Club
tel: 020 7352 2436
Yorkshire Terrier Club
01235 833171

Note
As committees change, so may their secretaries, which will make some of the telephone numbers printed here obsolete. In case of problems, phone The Kennel Club (see opposite) or Google the clubs on the Internet.

Magazines

Dog World
tel: 01233 621877
www.dogworld.co.uk
Dogs Monthly
tel: 0870 730 8433
www.dogsmonthly.co.uk
Dogs Today
tel: 01276 858860
www.dogstodaymagazine.co.uk
Our Dogs
tel: 0161 236 2660
www.ourdogs.co.uk
Your Dog BPG (Stamford) Ltd
tel: 01780 766199
www.yourdog.co.uk

Index

● Collins need to know?

**Look out for these recent titles in Collins' practical and accessible
need to know? series.**

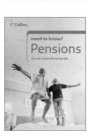  

Other titles in the series:

**To order any of these
titles, please telephone
0870 787 1732 quoting
reference 263H.
For further information
about all Collins books,
visit our website:
www.collins.co.uk**